Investing for a
Secure Retirement

Other MONEY *Books by Junius Ellis*

Money Adviser 1995

Making Money With Mutual Funds

Making the Most of Your Money Now

Your Best Money Moves Now

Investing for a Secure Retirement

Junius Ellis
And the Editors of MONEY

MONEY Books
Time Inc. Home Entertainment
1271 Avenue of the Americas
New York, NY 10020

If you have questions about this book or the MONEY Book Series, please call (800) 327-6388.

To order MONEY Magazine, please call (800) 633-9970.

Investing for a Secure Retirement

Editor: Junius Ellis
Designer: Laura Ierardi, LCI Design
Cover: Helene Elek; photo by Oki/Ortega

Time Inc. New Business Development

Director: David Gitow
Assistant Director: Stuart Hotchkiss
Fulfillment Director: Mary McGrade
Senior Manager: Pete Shapiro
Development Manager: John Sandklev
Production Manager: John Calvano
Operations Manager: Donna Miano
Assistant Manager: Alison Weiss
Marketing Assistant: Dawn Weland

Contents

1

Retire With All the Money You Need

*I*f you have given even a little thought to retirement, your mental picture probably includes an attractive home, perhaps overlooking a freshly mown fairway, two well-waxed cars in the garage, plenty of trips to sunny spots and a cluttered social calendar. That dream life is really not too different from the retirement fantasies of most middle-income members of your parents' generation. But there's an important difference now. Your dream most likely is clouded by fears that your savings eventually will run out, leaving you destitute and a burden to your children or the state.

Why weren't more people of your parents' generation haunted by those same nightmarish self-doubts before they retired? Simple. They were all but guaranteed a comfortable retirement by a succession of lucky breaks during their working years. In the 1950s and 1960s, family income after inflation rapidly rose more than 3.5% a year, on average, while housing costs for young families were low (about 16% of family income). Home prices outpaced inflation by four percentage points annually during the 1960s and five points annually during the mid-1980s. The return on stocks averaged an unprecedented 12% a year after inflation in the 1980s. Treasury bonds delivered fat 7% real returns. Meanwhile, Social Security payouts beat inflation by nearly three percentage points annually during your parents' working years.

Your generation can't expect the same ride. Wages, house prices and investment returns will probably grow at a comparatively slow to moderate pace during the

1990s and beyond. In fact, anyone who thinks there is no need to prepare early for retirement better think again. Just look at the statistics. Average life expectancy these days is around 76, up from 70 a generation ago. Yet the availability of employer-financed pensions is down 33%. The percentage of people age 55 to 64 who aren't working is 44%, compared with 38% in 1970. The age at which people now under 55 will be able to collect full Social Security benefits is 66, up from 65 today. All these changes have created a new set of rules that you must follow to be sure of retiring with all the money you need.

This chapter and others that follow will put you on the right course. We'll help you determine how much your retirement lifestyle will cost and what you will need to save to create your nest egg. We'll also show you the smartest way to invest your savings; assess a corporate severance or early retirement package; and choose where to live in your later years. But first you need to learn the new rules of the game.

Expect to live 30 years in retirement. That's nearly the life expectancy of today's 50-year-olds and may be more years than they spent working. A half-century ago they would have been lucky to reach 73. At the same time, the average retirement age has declined. Roughly 52% of workers now file for Social Security at age 62, up from 35% in 1978. But there is an increasing chance that a corporate buyout could force you to rewrite your retirement plan. Some 29% of firms surveyed by the American Management Association used voluntary separation packages to slash their payrolls during a recent 12-month period, up from 17% five years ago. The companies that used these programs included corporate giants like IBM that were once regarded as lifetime employers.

Don't rely on the firm or Feds. Financial planners often tell clients to think of retirement finances as a three-legged stool. One leg is Social Security. The second is your pension. And the third is personal savings. Retirees once could count on all three legs to remain steady. Today, however, Social Security and employer-financed pensions are getting shaky for many people. That means the third leg, personal savings, has to bear more weight.

Social Security will replace about 42% of wages if your earnings during your career averaged $21,800 a year but only about 27% if your average salary was $60,600. And this most sacred of middle-class entitlements is being chipped away. In recent years, the portion of your Social Security payments subject to federal income tax has climbed from 50% to 85% if your total income (including half of your Social Security payout) tops $44,000 for married couples and $34,000 for singles. The age at which you can expect to receive full Social Security benefits is also slated to rise, from 65 today to 66 in 2005 and 67 in 2022. With future outlays by the Social Security trust fund projected to outpace revenues by 2025, many retirement experts can foresee further cutbacks in the next decade or so. Among the likely options are another boost in the age for receiving benefits, a cut in beneficiaries' annual cost-of-living increases—or perhaps both.

If you're lucky, you'll be among the 40% of the work force whose Social Security checks will be supplemented by traditional defined-benefit pensions. These plans provide a fixed monthly payout, typically 30% of your final salary if you work 30 years or more. Even if your company offers a defined-benefit pension, you may have reason to worry about its safety. Underfunding at federally insured pension plans recently totaled $53 billion, up from $38 billion a year earlier, according to the federal Pension Benefit Guarantee Corporation. While these pensions are federally protected if your company folds or can't afford to stay in business without terminating its plan, you may not recoup all your promised pension benefits. And the reason is that federal insurance recently was capped at less than $31,000 a year.

Some companies have replaced traditional pensions with defined-contribution plans such as 401(k)s, which rely heavily on worker savings. Moreover, about half of workers with traditional pensions are covered by supplementary defined-contribution plans, up from roughly 33% in 1980. This reflects a basic shift from the view that the employer will take care of you to one where the employer will give you some retirement plans so you can take care of yourself. A 401(k) works well if you tend to job hop because you can take your retirement savings with you (provided that you've worked three to five years for your old employer). Traditional pensions aren't as portable and can penalize job hoppers because benefits depend on years of service. For a complete menu of your choices, check out our table "The Rundown on Retirement Plans" on page 12.

A 401(k), however, is less secure than a pension, which pays you a fixed amount each month, no matter how the markets perform. A 401(k)'s rate of return and your account's ultimate value are not guaranteed and partly depend on how astutely you invest. Also, 401(k)s tend to be invested too conservatively and earn lower investment returns than traditional pensions do. And many people spend their 401(k) savings when they change jobs, instead of hanging on to the money until retirement. Worse, companies tend to put less money in 401(k)s than in pensions. Employer contributions to defined-benefit plans run 10% to 12% of pay. Yet even in generous 401(k)s, employee contributions and employer matches might total 7% of pay. The chief reason is that younger and lower-paid workers can't afford to put much money in 401(k)s. The lower the amount, the less companies contribute.

Take charge of your future. Statistics suggest most workers aren't saving enough. America's 77 million baby boomers between the ages of 30 and 48 are now socking away just a third of what they need to maintain their standard of living in retirement, notes Stanford University economist Douglas Bernheim. People often put off saving for retirement so they can more easily achieve other goals, such as educating their children.

The Rundown on Retirement Plans

PLAN	AVAILABLE TO	BEST FOR	MAXIMUM CONTRIBUTION
401(k)	Employees of for-profit businesses	Everyone who qualifies	15% of salary, up to $9,240[1] in 1995
403(b)	Employees of nonprofit organizations	Everyone who qualifies	20% of gross salary or $9,500, whichever is less
IRA	Anyone with earned income	Those who don't have company pension plans or who have put the maximum into their company plans	100% of wages up to $2,000; $2,250 if joint with spouse
SEP	The self-employed and employees of small businesses	Self-employed person who is a sole proprietor	13% of net self-employment income, or $22,500, whichever is less[2]
PROFIT-SHARING KEOGH	The self-employed and employees of unincorporated small businesses	Small-business owner who is funding a plan for himself and employees	Same as SEP[2]
MONEY-PURCHASE KEOGH	Same as profit-sharing Keogh	Small-business owner who wants to shelter more than allowed by profit-sharing Keogh	20% of net self-employment income, or $30,000, whichever is less[2]
DEFINED-BENEFIT KEOGH	Same as profit-sharing Keogh	Self-employed person nearing retirement who needs to set aside a high percentage of income	Maximum needed to fund $120,000[1] annual benefit, or three years' average income, whichever is less[2]
VARIABLE ANNUITY	Anyone	Someone who has put the maximum into other plans and won't need the money for 10 years	None
FIXED ANNUITY	Anyone	Someone who has put the maximum into other plans and shuns risk	None

Notes: [1]Amount increases yearly with inflation rate. [2]Small-business owners fund the SEPs and Keoghs of their employees. [3]Percentage of employee's contribution [4]Some plans charge $20 to $30 annual administrative fees. [5]Surrender charges last six to eight years and typically decline by 1% a year. [6]All plans are subject to 10% income tax penalty, except in case of death or disability.

TAX BREAK ON CONTRIBUTIONS/ EARNINGS	MATCHING CONTRIBUTIONS	CHARGES/FEES	EARLY WITHDRAWAL[6]	NUMBER OF INVESTMENT OPTIONS
Yes/Yes	Anywhere from 0% to 100%,[3] but typically only up to 6% of salary	Depends on plan/annual expenses of 1% to 1.5% of assets[4]	Only in case of hardship	Three to 10, typically, depending on your employer's plan
Yes/Yes	Generally not available	Depends on plan/annual expenses of 1% to 3% of assets	Only in case of hardship and employee contributions only	One to 10, typically, depending on your employer's plan
Sometimes/Yes	None	Depends on investment/ zero to $50 annual fee	Always permitted	Nearly everything except real estate, collectibles and other hard assets
Yes/Yes	None	Depends on investment/ $10 to $30 a year	Always permitted	Same as IRA
Yes/Yes	None	Depends on investment/ up to $2,000 in annual administrative expenses	Always permitted	Unlimited
Yes/Yes	None	Same as profit-sharing Keogh	Always permitted	Unlimited
Yes/Yes	None	Depends on investment/ $2,000 to $4,000 annual expenses	Always permitted	Unlimited
No/Yes	None	6% to 8% surrender charges[5]/annual expenses of 2% to 2.2% of assets	Always permitted	Anywhere from one to 22, but typically nine
No/Yes	None	Surrender charges of 6% to 8%[5]	Always permitted	One

The longer you wait, however, the more you jeopardize your future well-being. Let's say that you're a 40-year-old with $20,000 in savings. If you put $2,000 a year in a 401(k) or other tax-deferred account, you'll accumulate $220,000 by age 62, assuming that you earn roughly an 8% annual return. If you wait five years longer to start saving, you'll have just $176,000.

Protect against inflation. Prices are expected to increase at a modest rate of around 3% this year. Yet you can't afford to gamble that inflation won't be considerably higher when you retire. Even at today's levels, price increases eventually take a big bite out of your benefit check. Over 15 years, 3% annual inflation will shrink the value of a $2,000-a-month pension by more than a third, while 4% inflation will cut it nearly in half. Most company pensions don't rise with annual inflation. Roughly a quarter of large firms surveyed by consultants Greenwich Associates have never increased retirement payouts, while another 28% haven't boosted benefit checks in at least seven years. Thus, early in retirement, a pension and Social Security might meet 60% to 80% of your needs. But in 12 or 15 years, as inflation eats into the value of your pension, they may provide only 40% of the income you need.

Keep expectations realistic. Over the past 10 years or so, earning double-digit annual returns has been a snap. Stocks in the Standard & Poor's 500 index returned a yearly average of 15%, and bonds maturing in five years gained about 11%, according to Ibbotson Associates, a Chicago investment research firm. Over the next five years, however, pension plan sponsors expect the S&P 500 to return only 9% annually and professionally managed bond funds just 7%. This means you'll have to save more to keep your retirement comfortable. In addition, you can't afford to play it too safe in investing your stash. About 27% of 401(k) assets lately were invested in low-risk, low-yielding GICs (guaranteed investment contracts), according to the consulting firm

Greenwich Associates. The better choice is stocks or stock funds, which will provide bigger returns over time and help keep your portfolio ahead of inflation.

Plan to keep on working. It's a mistake to think of retirement as a sudden exit from the work force. As many as half of all retirees take less demanding jobs to smooth their move from careers to retirement. By working in retirement, you enable your savings to keep compounding, and you delay the time you'll need to tap them, perhaps until age 62 or 65. Even more retirees are expected to work in the future because company early-out offers are forcing many employees to retire before they have built adequate savings. Still, retiring in comfort is clearly attainable. All you have to do is pay attention to the new rules and weigh the advice provided in subsequent chapters of this book.

▶ *Will Your Stash Last a Lifetime?*

Few working Americans are taking the steps needed to turn their retirement aspirations into reality. That's the sobering conclusion of a MONEY poll conducted with Oppenheimer Management, a Wall Street investment firm. Our poll found 73% of adults between the ages of 21 and 64 expect to retire comfortably and 74% plan to do so before 65. Yet less than half of those questioned are investing in assets that are likely to provide the money they will need. To cite one disturbing fact, nearly as many have purchased lottery tickets for retirement (39%) as have invested in stocks (43%).

So just how much money will be required to ease you on down the road? Take a 35-year-old man earning $50,000 who lacks a company pension or savings plan. He will need to amass the equivalent of $1 million over the next 30 years to retire comfortably at age 65 and support his lifestyle to age 90. Yet 73% of respondents estimated their investment needs to be lower (usually 33% to 50% lower). Moreover, three out of five believe they will be able to live on less than 70% of their pre-retirement income—the minimum amount, according to many experts. As a result, the typical American could end up with less than half the money he or she will need in retirement. What to do?

Get serious about planning. The nation's largest single age cohort, those 77 million baby boomers mentioned earlier, will not glide gently into their golden years unless they step up their savings pace. For one thing, they probably will receive a less generous stipend from Social Security than their parents' generation. By 2030, when most baby boomers will have retired, there will be only two workers paying into Social Security for every retiree, vs. about 3.2 to 1 today. Unless Washington beefs up Social Security financing or reduces its benefits, the system will likely start running in the red by the year 2025. Dwindling Social Security payments are not the only hurdle confronting baby boomers. Rising taxes are likely if Uncle Sam does not cut spending, notes economist Laurence Kotlikoff at Boston University. Says he: "If Congress doesn't take action to cut the deficit and slow health care spending, the baby boom generation could face tax hikes of as much as 40% in retirement." Increasing health care costs also seem certain for baby boomer retirees because, sooner or later, Congress must arrest the ballooning budget for Medicare and Medicaid (see our assessment in Chapter 7). Reduced corporate retirement benefits are likely too as businesses slash costs to remain competitive.

Affording a gracious retirement will be even more difficult for women because they tend to live longer than do men. Today's middle-aged female is likely to live to the age of 80, compared with 74 for her male counterpart. As a result, a woman needs a larger nest egg than a man to maintain the same level of investment income through retirement. At the same time, she may have a harder time accumulating what she needs. Women earn 30% less than men, on average, and they are also less likely to hold jobs that offer a company retirement plan. Single and divorced women are most at risk because they are less likely to share a spouse's benefits and full Social Security income. An Oppenheimer Management study found that the typical single woman who is in her thirties and lacks a pension will retire with only about 20% of the income she really needs.

It's never too soon to save. Consider this heartening example from a computer model designed by consulting firms WEFA Group and Arthur D. Little for Oppenheimer. Assume that a successful married couple in their early thirties earn $65,000, have a company pension and savings plan and get steady wage hikes of 1.5% above inflation each year. If inflation averages 3% for the next 30 years, they would earn the equivalent of $155,000 in today's dollars when they reach retirement at 67. Since their total outlays, including taxes, should be 20% to 30% lower in retirement, they could probably maintain their pre-retirement standard of living on an annual income equal to roughly $109,000 today. But look what happens if they save and invest like most Americans in their income bracket, putting away only 5% of their pretax salary each year. They shouldn't figure on generating more than $62,000 a year in income, including pension and Social Security. That would leave them $47,000 a year shy of what they need.

What would it take to prevent such a shortfall? Let's assume that the couple promptly reapportions their investment mix so that 84% of their assets is in stocks, vs. a norm of about 43%, and triple their savings to a conscientious 15% of income. According to WEFA and Arthur D. Little, their annual retirement income would nearly double to around $120,000. By putting more of their savings in tax-deferred accounts, such as 401(k)s, the couple could get a 100% increase in retirement income. The easiest way for most investors to accumulate such retirement riches is through mutual funds, which conveniently allow you to save regular amounts of money. Before you call for fund prospectuses, consider some of the following retirement fundamentals.

Double Check Your Social Security Benefits

Worried you won't get all the Social Security benefits you're entitled to? If not, maybe you should be. The Social Security Administration has disclosed the agency had a computer glitch that shortchanged 426,000 retirees by some $478 million over a 10-year period. Retirees had to wait up to six months to get reimbursed. But you can avoid a similar hassle by keeping tabs on what you have coming to you. Just call Social Security (800-772-1213) and ask for a copy of its Personal Earnings and Benefits Estimate Statement (PEBES) request form. Two to three weeks after submitting it, you'll receive a statement that totals your annual earnings to date and estimates your monthly Social Security benefit if you retire at age 62, 65 or 70.

If you're 60 or older, you can spare yourself making a telephone call. The folks at Social Security plan this year to send a benefits statement to everyone age 60 and over who isn't already getting checks from the agency. Then anyone who turns 60 will get a statement during the year of his or her 60th birthday. To avoid getting less than you deserve, you should request a PEBES every couple of years while you still have an accurate record of your recent earnings to compare it against. If you find a mistake, call 800-537-7005 to talk to a Social Security rep. Be prepared to send proof of your earnings to correct it. Officials hope that by the year 2000 the agency will start mailing to everyone a benefits statement every year. That's assuming, of course, Social Security benefits will still be available in the year 2000.

Scrutinize your budget. Do you really need to eat out three nights a week? Or even twice? Can you forgo that luxury coupe for the less costly sedan? And what about basic, money-saving moves such as shopping at warehouse clubs or improving your home's energy efficiency? Many families can save 10% or more just by cutting back on unnecessary expenditures. Before you start locking away that newfound money, however, make sure that you have built up an emergency cash reserve equivalent to three to six months' worth of expenses. You should keep that money in a safe place, such as a

CD (certificate of deposit) or money-market fund, where you can get your hands on it quickly without penalty. Once you get your savings plan under way, keep it in the groove by signing up for an automatic investing plan, authorizing your fund company to transfer a fixed amount every month from your bank account to funds of your choice. Most fund groups offer such automatic investing programs. And many of them will waive their investment minimum if you agree to make monthly contributions of as little as $50.

Shelter your nest egg. A tax-deferred savings plan can help speed you along the road to retirement wealth. You get an immediate tax deduction for your contribution. And, over the years, the effects of tax-deferred compounding can be awesome. Here's an example. If a 35-year-old earning $60,000 a year routinely contributes 6% of his salary to a taxable account earning 8% a year, he would have $185,744 by age 65 (assuming a 30% tax rate). If he were to invest that money in a tax-deferred account, he would amass a hefty $407,820. Even if he then withdrew the entire amount and paid taxes at a 30% rate on the proceeds, he would be ahead by 54%.

Many investors, however, don't take full advantage of their opportunities to shelter money. A survey of employers by accountant KPMG Peat Marwick found that only about 60% of eligible workers participate in 401(k)s even though 85% of employers match their contributions (typically 50¢ on the dollar up to a specified percentage of salary). Thus if your employer offers a 401(k), put in the maximum allowed. If you can't afford that much, at least put in enough to get the full matching amount offered by your company.

What if you don't have a company pension or retirement plan? Self-employed people can use so-called SEPs (Simplified Employee Pensions) that allow you to defer taxes on 13% of net business income, up to $22,500. A business owner can set up a Keogh plan. The three types are defined-benefit, profit-sharing and money-purchase. Depending on which you choose, you annually are allowed to contribute as little as you can afford or as much as $120,000. And don't overlook the merits of the humble IRA (Individual Retirement Account). Even though Congress has limited the deductibility of IRA deposits, you can still write off some or all of your contribution if you're not covered by a retirement plan at work or if you're married and have an adjusted gross income below $40,000 ($25,000 for single taxpayers). Even if you can't get an IRA deduction, you could still contribute $2,000 annually ($2,250 for married couples with one working spouse) and watch those earnings grow tax deferred.

Aim for stocks' higher returns. The most effective way to build your retirement portfolio is to invest in stocks rather than bonds and cash. Over nearly 70 years, stocks have returned an average of 10% annually, twice the 5% return for Treasury bonds. Cash investments such as Treasury bills merely matched the inflation rate at around 3%. To diversify properly, you will need to buy a variety of stocks and stock funds including blue chips for relatively stable returns and small companies for zippy gains that have averaged 12% annually over time. To add even more variety, spice up your mix with overseas stocks and funds. Many investment experts predict that foreign stock markets are likely to outpace the U.S. over the remainder of this decade by two to four percentage points a year. As for the fixed-income portion of your portfolio, consider a no-load fund that holds a mix of government and corporate bonds. High-income investors can earn fatter after-tax returns from municipal bonds and funds that specialize in them.

Your smooth-running retirement plan requires regular tune-ups, of course. You probably should attempt to re-evaluate your investments once a year. Then adjust your portfolio if needed, selling assets that have surged beyond your intended allocation and buying those that have slumped below. With a few adjustments and a bit of luck, you can still look forward to working primarily on reducing your handicap on the back nine.

2

Call It Quits
Earlier With
Confidence

*M*ost people, regardless of their age or career path, like to muse about retiring early and making leisure their primary pursuit. Yet more and more Americans are actually achieving that lofty goal. In fact, as life expectancy has risen, the age at which people retire has declined. The average age of retirement recently was around 61, down from 65 in 1970. Millions of wage slaves now are declaring their independence in their fifties and even forties. For them, retirement has come to mean almost anything except shuffling off to play another round of shuffleboard. Today's youthful retirees often run part-time businesses, volunteer at nonprofit institutions, take their hobbies seriously and travel the globe.

You probably have thought about how you would spend the time you earned after retiring early. Whatever your dream, the chances of attaining it are far better than you might imagine. Financial lures abound for people who cut loose while still young. A survey of large employers by the Wyatt Co., a benefits consulting firm, shows that 93% paid pensions to retirees at age 55 or earlier if they had served at least a specified number of years, usually 10 or 15. More people are eligible to receive pensions as a result of federal legislation that requires companies to cut vesting time from 10 years to either five or seven. Popular savings programs like 401(k)s and IRAs offer ways to build cash for an early retirement. And Social Security benefits may not be substantially reduced if you stop working before 62, the age when you can start getting the government checks.

Early retirement is not for everyone, of course. Many can't afford it. In one MONEY survey, having enough money for retirement was the No. 1 financial worry for people 35 to 49. You might not be able to get out early if you are facing tuition bills for your children's education well into your fifties. Your pension may be inadequate (or nonexistent) if you hopped jobs or work for a small firm. Others are psychologically unprepared for early retirement. You may not be ready either to give up the camaraderie of business associates or to spend a lot more time with your mate. One spouse may want to retire early but the other doesn't. More often, this scenario involves a woman who wants to stay on because she entered or re-entered the work force late or only recently landed a challenging job. Fear of boredom is genuine for those who can't figure out how they would occupy days without deadlines.

Traits for aspiring early retirees. For those intrigued by the concept of early retirement, the main prerequisites are preparation, creativity and dedication. You will have to reposition your investments while working to amass the pot needed at the retirement age you select. Quitting early obviously means that your savings must last longer than otherwise. Assuming a modest 4% annual return adjusted for inflation, someone planning to retire at 55 has to sock away $560,000 to collect $30,000 a year until age 90, compared with $468,000 for someone waiting until he is 65. The younger retiree also has 10 fewer years to accumulate that 20% additional cash reserve. Shrewd investing alone will not swing early retirement for everyone. There may well be some necessary trade-offs to weigh in the future, like telling your kids to set their sights on first-rate public colleges rather than expensive private schools. And you may have to make small sacrifices, such as cutting back on luxuries or entertainment, either before or after you retire.

The more creative you are earlier, the less spartan you will have to be later. Try to devise ways of building your own retirement annuity, not through an insurance company but through your own skills. Be sure to ask yourself: what could I do now that will bring in steady annual income after I retire? The answer might be honing a hobby that you will turn into a sideline business in retirement. It might be buying rental real estate today with a mortgage you will have paid off by the time you retire, thus positioning you to earn a tidy, positive cash flow. Or it might be picking up a new skill (discussed in greater detail later in this chapter).

The expertise that you gain could eventually become rewarding in all respects. But consulting, the most popular form of post-retirement entrepreneurism, ideally requires building contacts and a reputation before stepping down from your current job. Trying to market yourself as a consultant after you quit working can end up taking more time than you spent at your old job. If your dream involves running your own business, you had better get started now. Many service companies operate during nights and weekends and require no more start-up capital than the cost of a personal computer, laser printer, fax and telephone answering machine. Even if you are not contemplating a second career, you should start gearing up today to make sure you have enough money to carry you through retirement.

What you'll need to set aside. Deciding to retire early demands the right temperament as well as enough money. To help you gauge the former, take the quiz "Are You Really Ready to Retire?" later in this chapter. After all, a lot of people say that they expect to retire between the ages of 50 and 64. If so, they will likely live another 18 to 29 years on average. The most content early retirees are people who developed outside interests while working. Their identities were not wedded to their careers. If you can't come up with at least a dozen things you like to do, you're probably not a good candidate for early retirement. You must also determine whether you can swing it financially. For estimates of the costs and savings that are involved, fill out the worksheets beginning on pages 34 and 36.

Expect that your post-career expenses will equal 70% to 80% of your pre-retirement income. Next, figure how much you can safely expect from Social Security and your company pension. Social Security now replaces about a third of pre-retirement income, with the percentage falling as your salary climbs above $35,000. About 60% of retirees get pensions, which typically are based on your years of service and your salary for the last five years on the job. Ask your benefits department for an estimate of the pension you can expect at age 55 and at your company's normal retirement age, usually 65. Some employers will also calculate your pension starting on the date you hope to leave work.

Even though your pension check will almost always increase the longer you work, leaving your job before 65 may not cost as much as you think. Some experts argue that working past 60 can actually cut the total value of your future benefits in current dollars. Pension formulas typically increase your annual benefit more slowly after age 60. As a result, the only financial benefit you might receive from working an extra year would be that year's salary. Ask your benefits department what your pension will be if you leave at various ages, both on an annual basis and as a lump sum. Then have your accountant figure out when your pension will stop growing enough to make working longer worthwhile.

In recent years, many companies have offered special early retirement packages that sweeten pensions for employees who volunteer to accept these offers. Some of these deals are worth grabbing, but others are strikingly stingy. (We provide guidance on evaluating such arrangements later in this chapter.) Note, however, that an often overlooked pension penalty, introduced into tax law in the 1980s, may have the effect of discouraging some high earners from retiring early. Anyone retiring at 55 cannot collect more than a maximum annual pension benefit (the amount varies with your salary scale). This ceiling rises for people who retire at age 62 and those taking pensions starting at 65. Consult with your accountant or financial planner. Many companies may be able

Are You Really Ready To Retire?

While you may be all set for a financially secure retirement, you may not realize how much life after work can draw on your emotional reserves. If you suddenly find yourself with 40 or more hours a week of free time that you haven't adequately prepared for, you could be headed for trouble. These questions, based on the findings of gerontologists and psychologists, will help you determine how well prepared you are for the day when the alarm clock no longer rules. Answer each question that applies to you. Then tally the points assigned to each answer for your score. At the end, you can see what the specialists think.

	YES	NO
▷ Will you be able to cut back your hours at work gradually instead of all at once? *Change may exact a toll if it's too abrupt. Making the transition slowly gives you time to adjust at your own pace.*	+3	-3
▷ Are you married? *Being unmarried can reduce an individual's life expectancy more than smoking or being overweight.*	+4	-4
▷ If you're married, is the relationship satisfying? *Retirement can put a strain on your marriage. If you don't get along before you retire, chances are things will get worse afterward.*	+2	-2
▷ If your spouse is working, will he or she retire at about the same time as you? *An increasingly common problem occurs when the husband retires while his younger wife continues to work; it often reduces his self-esteem and creates confusion about household duties.*	+3	-3
▷ If you're not married, do you live with someone? *Although being in a satisfying marriage is the best way to overcome feelings of isolation, living with someone is a close second.*	+3	-3
▷ If you live alone, do you have daily contact with family or friends? *This is another substitute for a live-in companion.*	+2	-2
▷ Do you have at least one person outside of the office (for example, your spouse, a friend, even your banker or broker) in whom you can easily and comfortably confide? *Even if you rarely share intimacies with your pals, just the presence of a confidant can often be crucial to keeping your peace of mind.*	+4	-4

▶ Do you have a place at home or outside of it where you can have total privacy?   **+2**   **-2**
Together is fine up to a point. Everybody needs a retreat.

▶ Do you try not to hang around the office after the workday is over?   **+3**   **-3**
If you're spending too many hours at work, you may be dependent on the job for social life. Letting go will be hard for you.

▶ Have you made any new friends outside of work this year?   **+3**   **-3**
Don't make the mistake of assuming your work colleagues will still have time for you after you retire.

▶ Are you involved with community, church or cultural groups?   **+4**   **-4**
Such activities may prove to be the center of your post-work days. Don't wait until retirement to get involved outside your job.

▶ Do you schedule activities such as fishing trips, museum visits and picnics to fill up your free time?   **+3**   **-3**
Retirement may well be the first time in 40 years that you will control your own time. You should know how to plan your days without a boss looking over your shoulder.

▶ Have you taken part in an intellectual pursuit, such as attending a class or lecture, or a physical one, such as a competitive sport, in the past month?   **+2**   **-2**
Aim for a variety of activities. Just because you like fishing doesn't mean that after retirement you will enjoy it every day.

▶ Have you learned something new (say, a foreign language or computer skills) in the past five years?   **+2**   **-2**
Taking on new challenges shows an openness to change.

▶ Were you able to adjust easily when your children left home or during other periods of major change?   **+4**   **-4**
If you have been able to weather most of life's changes, you'll almost surely adjust well to retirement.

▶ Are you looking forward to retirement?   **+3**   **-3**
Your attitude can cast a shadow over everything. A negative one could become a self-fulfilling prophecy.

If you score 18 points or above, you are on solid footing. Between zero and 18, you have some catching up to do. Below zero, you need to work hard on improving your emotional preparation for retiring.

to skirt these ceilings by paying any higher obligations out of the company's reserves rather than pensions.

How to overhaul your portfolio. In your twenties and thirties, stocks or stock funds should make up as much as 70% to 80% of your retirement savings, with the balance in bond investments. As you approach early retirement you will want to start gradually reducing the stock portion until it hits a still sizable 50% when you quit. Why? With inflation and the long life expectancy of retirees, you need growth in your portfolio. Given steep top tax brackets of 36% and 39.6%, choosing the most tax-advantaged and cost-efficient vehicles for your retirement needs will also help your nest egg grow faster. Someone setting aside $4,000 a year for 35 years in a 401(k) plan earning an average of 8% annually will have $744,400 at retirement, compared with only $301,000 if he or she had put the same amount in taxable investments.

Why company plans are crucial. With capital gains taxed at 28%, upper-income investors with portfolios outside their sheltered retirement plans might put income-oriented investments into the plans and keep stocks that produce only capital gains outside. But your first retirement savings dollars should go into workplace plans such as 401(k)s. Yearly contributions of up to $9,240 (the maximum amount rises annually with inflation) are automatically taken out of your paycheck in pretax dollars, giving you the discipline of enforced savings and a tax cutter at the same time. Better yet, most companies that currently are offering 401(k)s match part of your contribution, producing an instant gain. If you work for a nonprofit organization or a school, your employer may offer a 403(b) plan or a tax-sheltered annuity in which you can stash cash.

You can shelter much more if you are self-employed. Some sole proprietors find a SEP (Simplified Employee Pension) is the solution. The maximum contribution is 13% of net business income, or $22,500, whichever is less. A business owner who's nearing retirement can sock away the most by way of a special defined-benefit Keogh that can be funded with contributions totaling up to $120,000 roughly. A small-business owner setting up a plan for employees as well may want to opt for a profit-sharing Keogh, whose annual contribution limit for the business owner is the same as a SEP's. The employer contributes to employees' accounts according to a formula based on their income. A profit-sharing Keogh is more flexible than a SEP, enabling you to vary contributions to employee accounts using such factors as age or length of service. If you want to invest even more for retirement for you and your staff, combine a profit-sharing Keogh with a money-purchase Keogh and put away an additional 7% of net earnings. But you'll have to commit to a set contribution level every year.

Don't forget IRAs and annuities. Since the demise of full deductibility for IRA contributions, these accounts have been overlooked by many investors. Yet IRAs should still be the second place for your retirement savings after company plans. You will qualify for a full or a partial IRA deduction if you don't have a company pension or if your adjusted gross income falls below $40,000 for a married couple or $25,000 for singles. Even if you don't get the write-off, you can still put up to $2,000 into a nondeductible IRA every year and get tax-deferred earnings. You should be forewarned, however, that there are paperwork hassles with nonde-ductible accounts. The solution is to hold deductible and nondeductible IRAs in separate accounts.

Variable and fixed annuities are also marketed as retirement vehicles because their investment earnings are tax deferred too. Variable ones let you put money into portfolios of stocks, bonds or cash. Fixed annuities pay a flat rate of interest. But unless you've already fully funded your workplace plans and IRA and are sure you will stay invested at least 10 years, think twice before putting money into annuities. First, you must put in after-tax dollars. You also could be clobbered by surren-der fees of as much as 8% of the amount you withdraw if you take money out within the first eight years, not to mention a 10% tax penalty on your accrued earnings if you want out before age 59.5.

The pain of future medical bills. Expenses
related to health care are likely to consume 15% to 20% of your income in retirement. To ease the burden, try to obtain comprehensive health insurance that will cover you from the day you retire until you turn 65 and qualify for Medicare. If you're among the most fortunate early retirees, your employer will let you keep your current coverage. Or, under the federal COBRA law, you can buy medical coverage through your company's group policy for 18 months at your employer's cost. Before your coverage runs out, look into joining your local HMO if it has a so-called open enrollment period (typically one month each year when it must accept all applicants). Also look for affordable private coverage, which is often cheaper than Blue Cross/Blue Shield if you're in good health.

Some good news on Social Security. It's a better
deal for early retirees than you might expect. True, your checks at 62 could be 20% smaller than if you waited to start receiving them at age 65. But a closer look at the numbers shows that the government actually promotes early retirement when computing Social Security benefits. Consider a 55-year-old male manager with a typical earnings history. If he retires now, in seven years he will begin getting a Social Security benefit of about $845 a month, in today's dollars. If he keeps working until 62, his monthly benefit will amount to about $900, only 7% more. Thus, if this man works seven more years, his extra payoff from Social Security will be peanuts.

The outlook for early retirement in the future is partly cloudy. Since a company plan will typically freeze your pension amount from the time you leave until its regular retirement date, inflation will melt a portion of your benefits. The aging of the U.S. population will also bring with it some ominous thunder for younger members of today's work force. The ratio of employees to retirees at many major corporations has slipped from about 15 to 1 in the 1970s to around 4 to 1 lately. That means as the baby-boom generation nears retirement at the turn of the century, companies will need to hang on to more employees. Early retirement packages may be curtailed lest businesses end up paying retirees almost as much as their employees. Moreover, Congress has approved changes that will snip Social Security benefits for early retirees in the next century. But by then, nearly a generation of Americans will have struggled throughout their youth for a chance to tell their boss to take the dumb job and shove it. Their reward will be an enticing opportunity to spend a full, idyllic third of their lives in well-plotted leisure. And that pleasure is something no government check can match.

▶ *Figuring How Much You Will Need*

You know you must save regularly and invest wisely to have enough money for a worry-free retirement, particularly an early one. But how much is enough? Well, let's assume that you will have a pension and Social Security. But those checks most likely will replace less than half your pre-retirement income. For investments to make up the difference of, say, another $20,000 a year that increases annually with inflation, you would need to retire with a $310,000 portfolio earning 8% pretax.

Instead of panicking about falling short or having to catch up, think instead about how your life will change when you leave work and then estimate the cost of that lifestyle. The traditional rule of thumb that retirees need 80% of their pre-retirement income may not hold true for you. You might consider it a hardship to have to make do with less just when you have time to enjoy the fruits of years of work and savings. Some frugal people may find that they need no more than 50% of their pre-retirement income. Health care aside, Americans over 65 spend 25% to 40% less than younger people do on food, clothing, housing, transportation and other everyday expenses. Whether to aim for 50% or 120% of your pre-retirement income depends on when you plan to stop working and how well you hope to live. Do you envision an early retirement of two homes and country clubs? Or quieter years making do with one car and fewer dinners out? Moreover, with retirement possibly lasting as long as 30 years, don't forget that your living costs will diminish as you age. Expenses tend to be highest for early retirees who travel extensively. Older ones typically spend less on such discretionary items as well as necessities (with the exception of health care).

These worksheets aren't a chore. To find out the dollars and cents of retirement, start with the worksheet "Estimate Your Future Costs Now" on page 34. Then let the worksheet titled "How Much You Must Sock Away" on page 36 guide you to an annual savings goal based on your anticipated retirement lifestyle, your current savings and your expected pension and Social Security benefit. For example, housing (line 1 in the worksheet "Estimate Your Future Costs Now") will continue to be your biggest expense even if you don't have a mortgage to pay now. Figure that your property taxes, homeowners insurance, utilities and upkeep will cost you no less than they do now unless you move to a smaller house or to a lower-cost area.

Your food costs (line 3) may decline 25% or so in retirement if you eat out less (obviously you won't buy lunch at work anymore). Transportation costs (line 4) will drop because you will no longer incur commuting expenses. And you may find that you don't need to replace a car so often or even keep two, especially later on. Unless your job never required pricey suits or dresses, you can expect to shave 20% to 35% off clothing costs (line 2). How much travel and entertainment costs (line 12) may change depends on your tastes. If early retirement means that you'll be going on more long trips, be sure to budget for them, since travel is often such retirees' single biggest new expense.

Chances are (you hope) you will have finished paying for your children's education by the time you retire. But think about whether you want to take courses yourself (line 7). You may also want to help your grown children buy a home or pay for their children's schooling. Members of the so-called sandwich generation may have to budget money for the care of their aging parents (line 16). As for loan payments (line 10), you should strive to reduce credit-card balances and other debt while you are still working.

Life insurance costs (line 8) usually go down or, in the case of disability insurance, disappear in retirement, since you typically will no longer have earnings from work to protect. Your income from investments, including those in retirement plans, doesn't need to be safeguarded by life insurance. Nor does your pension plan because federal law requires that a surviving spouse be paid a reduced benefit—unless he or she has formally waived it. On the other hand, you may decide that you need life insurance to provide liquidity in your estate or supplement a small pension for a surviving spouse.

Your biggest savings on taxes (line 15), assuming that you don't work in retirement, will be the Social Security and Medicare tax on wages. In addition, some states exempt some income from Social Security benefits and pensions from taxes. But don't look for many other breaks. Under the new federal tax law, as much as 85% of your Social Security benefits may be taxable, depending on your overall income.

Trying to predict medical expenses (line 9) is tough because you don't know what health problems you may face or the outcome of the health reform debate. Nonetheless, for purposes of the worksheet, assume that health care costs could be higher. In addition, early retirees may face higher medical costs until they qualify for Medicare at 65 if they have to buy their own insurance, which can cost up to $5,000 a year. You also should figure on your health costs staying high after 65 because of higher out-of-pocket medical expenses and insurance premiums. For example, a supplemental Medicare policy could run as

Estimate Your Future Costs Now

▶ **Line 1:** If you pay off your mortgage and take care of all necessary maintenance problems before you retire, housing costs should drop by as much as 25% to 30%. Count on even more shrinkage if you sell your house and buy a smaller one. Condominium owners and renters should factor in the expense of periodic maintenance and rent increases. And anyone who plans to spend more time at home should anticipate paying higher utilities charges.

▶ **Line 2:** Financial planners estimate that if you are moving from business suits to jeans, you can expect to reduce clothing expenses by 20% to 35%.

▶ **Line 4:** Scratch commuting costs. Other transportation expenses will increase if you intend to be very active. Planners recommend that two-car couples keep both autos during retirement, especially if both are fairly active.

▶ **Line 6:** Most people keep giving the same amounts to charitable, political and educational institutions, as well as to family members outside the immediate household. But the overall figure drops, usually by the amount you used to give at the office.

▶ **Line 7:** If your kids will be grown by the time you retire, you can eliminate education expenses, unless you plan to help pay your grandchildren's college bills. And if you intend to return to school yourself, check into reduced tuition costs for senior citizens.

▶ **Line 8:** There will be little change in your payout for property, personal liability and automobile insurance. But retirees can generally reduce their life insurance coverage by at least 50% or, if their spouses are fully provided for under their pension plan, eliminate the policy altogether.

▶ **Line 9:** If you are currently covered by a company health plan, expect medical and dental costs to spurt by about 50% because of increased illnesses combined with reduced insurance coverage. Medicare pays part of doctors' fees and hospital bills. Check your company's coverage for retirees.

▶ **Line 10:** Most retirement experts say you should plan to be debt-free by the time you retire, thereby eliminating loan repayment expenses.

▶ **Line 12:** How much you continue to spend for entertainment depends on how active you are. Expect such expenditures to rise an average of about 20% during your retirement.

▶ **Line 13:** You probably should be prepared to budget for higher veterinary bills if you will have an aging dog, cat or other pet.

▶ **Line 14:** While your contributions to pension plans cease at retirement, many financial planners encourage clients to continue setting aside about 10% of their income as a hedge against inflation.

▶ **Line 15:** If you don't work, it's farewell to Social Security (FICA) taxes. Also check laws in your state because some don't tax income from retirement plans. The conventional wisdom that you will be in a lower tax bracket after retirement is no longer true for high earners. You will be taxed on up to 50% of your Social Security benefits if the total of your adjusted gross income, nontaxable interest, and half your Social Security benefits exceeds $25,000 ($32,000 if you are married). If that total is over $34,000 ($44,000 for married couples), you'll owe tax on up to 85% of Social Security benefits.

▶ **Line 16:** With more adult kids expecting some form of financial help from Mom and Dad and Americans' increasing longevity, you could be contributing to the down payment on a child's first house while paying for a parent's nursing home.

The figure for total current expenditures should equal approximately 100% of your current before-tax income. By dividing your total expenditures at retirement by your current gross income, you will arrive at the percentage of your current income that you will need to live comfortably in retirement.

EXPENDITURES	AT RETIREMENT	CURRENT YEAR
1. Housing. Rent or mortgage payments, property taxes, utilities (gas, oil, electricity and water), telephone, home furnishings, household services, maintenance, improvements	_____	_____
2. Clothing. Purchases and cleaning	_____	_____
3. Food. (including tobacco and alcohol)	_____	_____
4. Transportation. Car repair and maintenance, installment payments, gas, commuting costs, other	_____	_____
5. Gifts.	_____	_____
6. Contributions.	_____	_____
7. Education.	_____	_____
8. Insurance. Life, medical, auto, property, liability	_____	_____
9. Medical and dental care. Premiums, deductible and out-of-pocket costs	_____	_____
10. Loan repayment costs.	_____	_____
11. Personal care. Grooming, health club, other	_____	_____
12. Entertainment. Vacations, dining out, movies, plays, concerts, sports events, cable TV, videocassettes, entertaining, sports, hobbies, other	_____	_____
13. Pet expenses.	_____	_____
14. Investments and retirement savings. Contribution to company plans, IRAs, Keoghs, SEPs and other investments	_____	_____
15. Taxes. Federal, FICA, state, local	_____	_____
16. Support of relatives.	_____	_____
Total Expenditures. (add lines 1 through 16)	_____	_____
Total Current Expenditures Divided by Current Gross Income.	_____	_____
Total Expenditures at Retirement Divided by Current Gross Income.	_____	_____

How Much You Must Sock Away

The worksheet at right will tell you how much you need to start saving now to hold on to your standard of living in retirement. The multipliers that are used in lines 7, 9 and 11 allow for inflation by assuming that your investments will grow at three percentage points over the inflation rate, before and after retirement. This keeps all of the figures in today's dollars.

▶ **Line 3:** You and your spouse can easily keep tabs on what you have coming to you from Social Security. Just call Social Security (800-772-1213) and ask for a copy of its Personal Earnings and Benefits Estimate Statement (PEBES) request form. Two to three weeks after submitting it to the agency, you should get a free statement that notes your annual earnings to date and estimates your monthly Social Security benefit if you decided to retire at age 62, 65 or 70. If you're 60 or older, you can spare yourself a telephone call. The folks at Social Security plan this year to send a benefits statement to everyone age 60 and over who isn't already getting checks from the agency. Then, anyone who turns 60 will get a statement during the year of his or her 60th birthday.

▶ **Line 4:** Your company benefits department may be able to estimate your pension. Make sure the estimate assumes that you continue working until your retirement age at your current salary. That will understate your likely eventual payout but will keep the figure in today's dollars.

▶ **Line 7:** The multipliers in column A incorporate the cautious assumption that men will live to 90 and women to 94—longer than 85% of them do now. Single men should use the multiplier under "men." Women and married couples should use the one under "women," since wives usually outlive their husbands.

▶ **Line 8:** Your personal retirement portfolio includes any investments that you have specifically earmarked for retirement, aside from your IRA or Keogh. For your employer-sponsored savings plans, check the most recent statement from your 401(k), profit-sharing, thrift or stock ownership plan and total your vested balance in each.

▶ **Line 12:** You should consult the annual statement from these plans to find and total the amount that your company contributed on your behalf to each of the plans last year. Then enter the total.

AGE AT WHICH YOU EXPECT TO RETIRE	MULTIPLIER A	
	MEN	WOMEN
55	22.1	23.5
56	21.8	23.2
57	21.4	22.8
58	21.0	22.5
59	20.6	22.1
60	20.2	21.8
61	19.8	21.4
62	19.3	21.0
63	18.9	20.6
64	18.4	20.2
65	17.9	19.8
66	17.4	19.3
67	16.9	18.9

TIME UNTIL YOU EXPECT TO RETIRE	MULTIPLIER B	MULTIPLIER C
1 year	1.03	1.000
3 years	1.09	.324
5 years	1.16	.188
7 years	1.23	.131
9 years	1.30	.098
11 years	1.38	.078
13 years	1.47	.064
15 years	1.56	.054
20 years	1.81	.037

1. Current gross income _____

2. Annual income needed in retirement, in today's dollars (70% of line 1) _____

3. Annual Social Security retirement benefits _____

4. Annual pension benefits _____

5. Guaranteed annual retirement income (line 3 plus line 4) _____

6. Additional retirement income needed (line 2 minus line 5) _____

7. Capital required to provide additional retirement income (line 6 times multiplier from column A at left) _____

8. Amount you have saved already

_____ + _____ + _____ = _____

personal retirement portfolio   IRA/Keogh   employer-sponsored savings plans   total savings

9. What your current investments will have grown to by the time you retire (total from line 8 times multiplier from column B at left) _____

10. Additional retirement capital required (line 7 minus line 9) _____

11. Total annual savings still needed (line 10 times multiplier, column C at left) _____

12. Annual employer contributions to your company savings plans _____

13. Amount you need to set aside each year (line 11 minus line 12) _____

much as $3,500 a year. And don't forget routine dental costs, which may mount with age and are unlikely to be covered by your insurance company.

Don't expect to stop saving. That's because saving is one of the only ways you can counteract inflation. Experts recommend that you plan to put aside up to 10% of your income annually in the first few years after you stop working. Moreover, in your early retirement years, you might take a part-time job to supplement your income from pensions and taxable investments. That way your tax-deferred accounts can keep on growing to help cover unexpected costs and provide income when you stop working altogether.

Now fill out the worksheet titled "How Much You Must Sock Away" to determine the amount you should save every year until you finally stop working. As the line-by-line instructions specify, you'll need estimates of your future Social Security benefit and your company pension. If you're close to retirement, your firm's benefits department may be willing to project a pension benefit that has been based on your planned retirement age, which will be more accurate than one based on your current years of service.

You will likely find that your pension and Social Security won't equal your expected retirement living costs. If you retired last year and were earning $60,600, the maximum wage that was covered by Social Security, your government benefit would have replaced about 27% of that amount. If you had earned $85,000, that Social Security benefit would have made up only about 19%. Note that early retirees now collect 80% of the full benefit if they start receiving checks at age 62. That percentage will decline to 75% in 2005 and 70% in 2022 as the age for full benefits rises. Don't count on your pension to pick up what Social Security doesn't cover. What you collect will be based on years of service and your salary over the past three to five years that you were on the job. Pensions typically replace about 30% of pre-retirement salary and rarely increase with inflation.

▶ How to Size Up a Company Offer

Several years ago, Michael Yendrzeski and 5,800 other Eastman Kodak employees as young as 47 received buyout offers they felt they couldn't refuse. The package included full pensions, health insurance for life, two weeks' salary for each year of service and bridge payments of as much as $900 a month until they could collect Social Security at 62. Yendrzeski, then 50, walked away from his job as a senior product engineer with $400,000 counting a $900-a-month bridge benefit. With Michael pulling down $900 or so a week as a consultant and his wife Deborah earning $25,000 a year as a dental hygienist, the couple's annual income recently totaled nearly $73,000. And the lump sum from Kodak is quietly growing in a tax-deferred IRA. "We're now living just as well as ever but our total assets have tripled," explains Yendrzeski. "For me, the only question was, why would anyone not do this?"

That same question now haunts the Kodak workers who didn't take the offer. Two years later, Kodak began involuntary layoffs that aim to reduce its work force by 10,000. Those getting the ax received a far less generous good-bye than the 1991 departees. The deal included up to a year of severance but no pension boosts and health insurance for just four months.

There's a costly lesson for employees of Kodak and other big corporations in the enduring era of buyouts. If you're offered a package that looks reasonable, take the money and run because a less generous deal may come your way in a year or two. And it may not be voluntary. How likely are you to face a buyout? If you're over 55 and a manager in a shrinking industry such as manufacturing or retailing, employment experts rate your chances at about one in four.

Companies generally use two types. First are early retirement offers made to workers of 55 and over. If you get one and you're lucky, it will include an enhanced pension such as Yendrzeski's. On the other hand, you might be presented with one that doesn't give you a bridge to Social Security or excludes health insurance. The number of downsizing companies that offer early retirement incentives fluctuates widely from year to year. One reason is that these packages are expensive and must conform to elaborate federal nondiscrimination rules. As a cheaper alternative, employees of all ages are offered arrangements called voluntary separation packages. They typically add up to enough to tide a family over for a year at most.

Accepting either variety of buyout may make sense. First, however, you need to explore these key issues to determine whether the offer works in your favor.

What choices you may encounter. Under federal law, you can't be forced to take a package. But the law doesn't prevent an employer from later firing you, eliminating your job, demoting you, cutting your pay or otherwise making you wish that you had taken the buyout. So before turning it down, make sure your company wants you to stay. For example, if your boss seems happy with your performance and the offer is company-wide, you can probably afford to ignore it. If your boss is unhappy, or the offer is targeted at a specific division or department, you ought to give it serious thought. Another tension heightener is that you usually won't have more than two or three months to think things over. If you feel you must take the package but worry that you aren't financially prepared to leave work, you might read the crash-course book *Retirement: Ready or Not* by New York financial planner Lee Rosenberg.

What to look for in early-out deals. In an offer extended only to employees older than 50 or 55, an employer will usually adjust your pension to make it bigger than you'd otherwise deserve. We're talking about a traditional defined-benefit pension. Vested money in a profit-sharing or 401(k) savings plan will be yours whenever you leave work. The most common pension adjustment technique is to add several years to your age, length of service or both so as to fatten your payout. Your company may also have elected to provide a financial bridge to Social Security that equals some or all of the payments you will be eligible to receive from the government starting at 62. If you're bridged from age 60, for example, the effect is like starting to get your Social Security checks two years early.

What to look for in separation deals. Here you get only a cash incentive to leave, usually two or three weeks' salary for each year of your service, up to a maximum of a year's pay. A poor package might include only a week of pay for each year of service, or the offer might top out at 26 weeks and give you no health insurance. A good deal might offer as much as a month of pay per year plus health insurance for a year or more. In addition, if you're vested in your company's pension plan, you'll get it when you reach your employer's regular retirement age.

What to make of a generous offer. Having to decide whether to volunteer for a package comes down to this question—can you afford to retire? Even if the buyout, plus your other assets, gives you enough to meet your short-term needs, you may not be able to finance all of your retirement years, particularly if your prospects for getting another job are dim. And bear in mind that even the most generous deal won't deliver the same income you would get by staying on until normal retirement. One reason is that your pension rises with your salary. After retirement, however, most pensions don't keep up with inflation. (For details, see "When It Pays to Stay on the Job" on page 42.)

What about health coverage. While early retirement offers often include lifetime health insurance, voluntary severances typically don't. But you have the right to continue in your firm's medical plan for 18 months at your own expense. After that, you'll have to buy private coverage. This can cost as much as $5,000 a year, if

When It Pays to Stay on the Job

Even a generous early-out package won't make up for the bigger pension you'd earn by staying on the job. In the table below, we analyze an offer to a 55-year-old who earns $50,000 and has worked 20 years for a company. The package adds five years to both his age and years of service, which gives him the pension he would normally get at 60, and pays him an additional $6,800 for seven years. That's two-thirds of his expected Social Security benefit at 62. The table shows that if he turns down the deal and works until 60 or 62, he will boost his annual retirement income by as much as $8,890. Here are the components of that figure: about $6,890 in additional pension, some $1,600 from his fatter 401(k) plan and $400 from his higher Social Security benefit.

Age	Income with retirement at 55 without the package	Income with retirement at 55 with the package	Income with retirement at age 60	Income with retirement at age 62
55	$9,073	$21,177	$51,500	$51,500
56	9,073	21,177	53,000	53,000
57	9,073	21,177	54,600	54,600
58	9,073	21,177	56,300	56,300
59	9,073	21,177	58,000	58,000
60	9,073	21,177	17,354	59,700
61	9,073	21,177	17,354	61,500
62[1]	19,273	24,577	27,754	33,468
63	19,273	24,577	27,754	33,468
64	19,273	24,577	27,754	33,468
65	19,273	24,577	27,754	33,468

Note: The table assumes that the employee's pension is based on his five highest years of earnings, that he gets 3% annual pay hikes, and that he contributes 3% of salary to his 401(k), which he annuitizes at retirement. [1]Social Security kicks in. **Source:** Kwasha Lipton you're over 50, until Medicare kicks in at 65. If you're not healthy, you may not be able to obtain coverage.

What about income in retirement. If you have prospects of another job or plan to start your own business, you may have more latitude to accept an offer that isn't perfect, particularly if you have a working spouse. Consider the example of LaMarr Hamilton, 54, of Vista, Calif. He had worked as an IBM computer technician for 26 years when he took a voluntary severance package. IBM offered him a year's salary of $45,000 plus full health, dental and life insurance. At 55, Hamilton could start collecting a $1,380-a-month pension. If he died before his wife Sally, 52, she would receive $700 a month for life. Bolstered by $350,000 in assets, Sally's $20,000 income as a medical secretary and the guarantee of another job, LaMarr decided to take the offer. Now earning $43,000 as a computer technician for a retailer, he has invested much of his buyout cash in stocks. He expects his investments to grow to $1.5 million by 2002, enabling him to retire early with an income of at least $3,000 a month. That's 80% of his old IBM salary.

▶ *Do You Want a Post-Job Job?*

Career switching and part-time employment are the rage among retirees who are seeking an escape from the paralyzing boredom that afflicts so many of their peers. What with longer, healthier lives and earlier, richer retirements, Americans face the prospect of decades of active, useful living after they receive the golden handshake. What sensible person whose life has largely been defined by the workplace would want to laze through so many potentially fruitful years? Here are answers to some of the first questions you are apt to ask about that next big step.

Why work after I retire? To begin with, you may have no other choice. Inflation, poor planning and an inadequate company pension may force the issue. And even if you don't need a job to make ends meet, you may decide that you want one just to help you keep active and healthy. Those are both benefits that become increasingly more crucial as you get older.

Does it pay to keep working? If you're well off, you could wind up losing money by working. Social Security and tax code provisions penalize people who earn too much in retirement. If you're 62 to 64, you couldn't have earned more than $8,040 last year and still received your full Social Security check. The penalty for earning more is a stiff 50¢ deducted from your benefit for each dollar in salary that you made above $8,040. Retirees age 65 or older could have earned as much as $11,160 and collected full benefits. The penalty for earning more is 33¢ on each additional dollar. (The dollar limits increase annually with inflation.) After 70, there's no benefit loss no matter how much you make. In addition, you are taxed on up to 50% of your Social Security benefits if the total of your adjusted gross income, non-taxable interest, and half your Social Security benefits exceeds $25,000 ($32,000 if you are married). If that total exceeds $34,000 ($44,000 for couples), you owe tax on up to 85% of your benefits. If you keep working past 65, your benefits will rise by a certain percentage each year until age 70. These increases range from 3% to 8% depending on the year of your birth.

How should I plan another career? Start as soon as you can—certainly well before you call it quits. If you want to change fields, you should begin planning at least five years before you retire. This will give you time to take classes and meet people in your field of interest. Even if you want to stay in the same field, it's a good idea to start research on potential employers a year before your planned retirement.

What's the best way to find a job? Most career counselors answer this question with the buzz word networking. Make a list of friends, relatives, business relations, old school chums and even distant acquaintances who may be able to help you find a job, whether it is in your old field or a new one. You can often make useful contacts at career seminars or by joining professional organizations. If you don't know anyone at a company that you are interested in, try to find out the name of the person who has the power to hire you. Look in the *Reference Book of Corporate Managements* or in the *Standard & Poor's Register* (both are available at most libraries). Or phone the personnel department at the company. Then write a letter to that executive detailing your skills and interests. After a week or so, follow up with a phone call. Be cordial but persistent. You typically will have to be interviewed by scores of people, and it may take up to a year before a job offer materializes.

Are pensioners paid less? The practice of offering lower pay to workers who already are receiving pensions exists at many companies, but habits are changing. Federal law protects older job seekers from arbitrary hiring and salary discrimination. And employers are coming to appreciate that older workers are usually well worth full pay. If you are asked your salary expectations, be assertive. To protect yourself from being shortchanged, find out what the average salary is for the position you want. Career counselors or library research can help. Should you meet the job qualifications for a position in your old field, it's only fair that you should request the middle to high end of the salary range. If you are changing fields and need additional training, you should expect your salary to be at the low end of the scale.

Should I start a business? Probably not. While independence sounds exhilarating, don't forget that 66% of small businesses fail within five years, often because of poor planning or lack of funds. Before you embark on what could be a financially and emotionally devastating experience, ask yourself the following questions (more than one or two nays should give you pause). Do I have a product or service that is really needed? Do I have financial backing or money of my own that I can afford to lose? Am I happy working alone? Most telling, do I consider myself a risk taker? Someone who's been a middle manager at the same company for 30 years may not have what it takes to become an entrepreneur. If you are convinced that you are one, you should seek advice from people who have started their own businesses. The Service Corps of Retired Executives, which is sponsored by the Small Business Administration, provides free advice on starting your own business. Look for it in the phone book under U.S. Government/SBA/SCORE.

What about training and placement? Your first and best source is your employer. That's because more and more companies offer job planning and counseling. Another option is to phone your state job training or employment service (look in the phone book under State Government Offices). Many have listings for older workers or can at least direct you to placement services in your area. Private career counselors provide occupational testing, one-on-one counseling and training in job-search skills. But if your employer doesn't pay the fees for you, be prepared for charges that can run into the thousands. Another excellent source of help is the growing number of nonprofit organizations that are set up to assist older workers. You can write for information about nonpaying consulting work to the National Executive Service Corps (257 Park Avenue South, New York, N.Y. 10010), a volunteer placement service for retired executives. Small and medium-size firms recruit via its Senior Career Planning & Placement Service.

Can I try out a career? If you don't need to work for money, you should explore the field of volunteering. Often this can later turn into a paid job. There's a big advantage to starting this way. You can set your own schedule and contribute your time to a cause that may give you great satisfaction. Volunteer opportunities abound in hospitals, day care centers, libraries, schools and many other community or charitable organizations.

3

Sure Ways to Invest for Your Future

*E*ven a generous company pension and savings plan, coupled with the maximum Social Security benefit, probably won't provide you with enough income for a care-free retirement. To keep your standard of living from dropping after you leave work, you must buttress your retirement savings with your own investments. And you can't just sock your money away. You have to invest it wisely. Let's assume that you had the discipline to save $500 a month for 30 years and stashed it all in a riskless money-market fund. If your money earned 6.5% annually, on average, you would have accumulated about $553,000. Now let's say that you put your money instead into a growth-minded mix of mostly stocks and some bonds (or mutual funds that invest in these securities). Assuming an average return approaching 10% a year, an achievable one for such a portfolio over three decades, you would have ended up with a cool $1 million bundle. The price for nearly doubling your return, however, is much greater uncertainty in the short run.With only a moderately risky growth portfolio, you still should be prepared to ride out market drops that could be as grim as 20% in the course of several months or even weeks.

Are you game? If so, you should be able to put any reasonable retirement dream within reach by following the investing strategies outlined in this chapter. Whether you are starting or unscrambling your nest egg, the key decisions in the years ahead will hinge mainly on how old you are, where your financial assets currently are concentrated, your outlook for the economy and—most important—your tolerance for risk. The prevailing moods of the stock and bond markets are just two of the factors you must weigh in deploying your money. You should also make gradual adjustments in your mix of assets to correspond with your changing needs for capital growth, steady income or a combination of the two, particularly as you draw nearer to the day when you call it a career.

▶ *Zero in on Your Comfort Zone*

Regardless of your age or how well you have diversified your portfolio, the most important challenge is to find your comfort zone and to know that it will change as your temples gray and your career progresses. Astute asset allocation begins with a careful analysis of your investments and other aspects of your financial life to determine how each of these affects your exposure to the following types of risk.

▶ **Inflation risk.** Rising prices will reduce the purchasing power of an investment. An annual inflation rate of 5% over 15 years will cut the value of $1,000 to $480. Overcautious investors who hoard assets in low-yielding investments such as savings accounts and money-market funds may not earn enough to outpace rising prices. Rising inflation also erodes the value of future income generated by investments with fixed payments, most notably long-term bonds.

▶ **Interest-rate risk.** Rising interest rates will cause investments to drop in price. Higher rates make yields on existing bonds less attractive, so their market values decline. Rising rates also hurt stocks by making their dividend yields less appealing. People who invest borrowed money through margin accounts or have other types of floating-rate debt increase their risk because higher interest rates cut into their net profits.

► **Economic risk.** Slower growth in the economy will cause investments to fall in price. Shares of small growth companies may shrink because they require a booming economy to sustain their robust earnings gains. Cyclical companies, such as automakers and chemical producers, can't easily cut costs during a recession. So their shares may nosedive. Economic downturns can also undercut junk bonds issued by financially weak firms that might default.

► **Market risk.** This includes such factors as political developments and Wall Street fads that can batter investment markets. Tax law changes, trade agreements, program trading and the quirks of investor psychology all contribute to market risk, which has accounted for much of the stock market's day-to-day volatility. Gold also carries considerable market risk because its price moves sharply when political or military upheavals in other countries encourage the flight of capital.

► **Specific risk.** This covers occurrences that may affect only a particular company or industry. Poor management or bad luck can dampen earnings or even bankrupt a company. And high-flying growth stocks are particularly vulnerable to earnings disappointments. Individuals take on a high degree of specific risk when they buy stock in a firm with a heavy debt burden or invest in specialty stock funds, often called sector funds because they concentrate their holdings in a single industry such as energy. Specific risk also includes the chance that government regulation will harm a particular group of companies.

► *Take an Inventory of Your Assets*

After uncovering the major risks in your portfolio, you can redeploy assets to reduce your exposure. Don't limit your inventory to investments that are kept in a brokerage account. Your earning power probably is by far your most valuable asset; equity in a home may come next. Many investors also have substantial assets invested in company pension plans or insurance policies with significant cash values. And entrepreneurs should take a close reading of the risks that threaten the value of their small business.

Risk tends to creep up on even vigilant investors. Your holdings in a retirement plan may grow more quickly than you realize, particularly if you make regular contributions or reinvest your returns. But with this success comes a problem. Growth in one asset can throw a portfolio out of balance if other investments don't keep up. If a prolonged bull market boosts the value of your stockholdings, you may need to sell some shares to restore the balance between stocks and other assets. Similarly, when a single stock does extremely well, you have to consider whether it's time to shed some shares. Be especially wary of loading up on your company's stock through retirement and savings plans. If the company runs into trouble, both your job and your stock could be endangered at the same time. If you live in a one-company town, the value of your home may also be tied to the fortunes of that firm. To gauge your own situation, you will need to conduct a survey of your investments and other aspects of your finances. Here's a rundown of the strengths and weaknesses of various assets.

Stocks and stock funds. They are vulnerable to the possibility that skittish investors will panic for some reason and drive share prices down en masse (an example of market risk). But risks related to inflation, interest rates or economic growth may vary considerably from stock to stock. For example, a sharp increase in the inflation rate depresses stock prices because it may reduce the purchasing power of future dividends to shareholders. What's more, inflation generally coincides with higher interest rates, which draw investors from stocks to bonds. Because firms such as retailers, consumer product

Rate Your Retirement Portfolio's Risk

Most people shield some of their investments against different types of risk. But few balance all of their assets so that they are well protected. This quiz can help you identify your points of vulnerability. With each question, you will accumulate points for one or more of the five major investment risks that are described in the main text. Write the points in the boxes below. Then total the points for each risk and interpret your scores as follows. Fewer than five points is low. Five to 10 points is moderate. Above 10 points is high. While you may want to vary your exposure to different categories of risk, depending on your personal circumstances and outlook for the financial markets, any score that comes in above 10 points should set off alarm bells.

Once you have identified vulnerabilities, you can take steps to shore up your defenses. Say that you score high for inflation risk and low for market risk. You might balance your portfolio better by switching some cash from money-market funds to real estate, stocks or gold. While your risk of a temporary decline in the value of your portfolio will increase, you will have a better chance of outpacing inflation over the long term.

In answering the questions, don't make the mistake of overlooking 401(k) accounts, IRAs or any other savings or deferred-compensation plans. It may be difficult to pin down the value of some assets. For instance, you may have a universal life policy with an important investment component. Just make the best estimates that you can. It isn't necessary to be exact. But it is important that your inventory be as complete as possible.

Questions

	INFLATION RISK	INTEREST-RATE RISK	ECONOMIC RISK	MARKET RISK	SPECIFIC RISK
► Are your assets diversified among fewer than four of these five categories—stocks, real estate, gold, bonds and cash? If yes, score one point for each risk.					
► Are more than 35% of your assets invested in any one of the five categories? If yes, score one point for each risk.					
► Is at least 10% of your portfolio in assets such as gold, natural-resource stocks or high-grade collectibles such as rare stamps? If no, score one point for inflation risk.					
► Is at least 30% of your portfolio in investments such as growth stocks and real estate, which are likely to produce long-term capital gains that can outpace inflation? If no, score two points for inflation risk.					
► Are your real estate and gold investments held primarily in assets such as gold-mining shares and REITs (real estate investment trusts), which tend to fluctuate with the stock market? If yes, score one point for market risk.					
► Do you generally keep at least 15% of your portfolio in cash equivalents such as Treasury bills or money-market funds? If no, score two points for interest-rate risk.					
► Is more than 30% of your portfolio composed of assets such as long-term government bonds, CDs (certificates of deposit) or annuities that promise to pay investors fixed payments over a period of many years? If yes, then score three points each for inflation and interest-rate risk.					

	INFLATION RISK	INTEREST-RATE RISK	ECONOMIC RISK	MARKET RISK	SPECIFIC RISK
▶ Do highly volatile zero-coupon bonds account for more than 30% of your fixed-income assets? If yes, score two points each for inflation and interest-rate risk.					
▶ Do small growth stocks or junk bonds, which may fall sharply in a recession, account for more than 25% of your portfolio? If yes, score three points for economic risk.					
▶ Do you switch money among different assets to try and catch the highs and lows of different investment markets? If yes, score two points for market risk.					
▶ Do you use dollar cost averaging or a similar plan that involves adding money to your investment portfolio at regular intervals? If no, score two points for market risk.					
▶ Is more than 20% of your portfolio concentrated in a single industry? If yes, score three points each for economic risk, market risk and specific risk.					
▶ Do stocks or bonds issued by one company (including the one that you work for) or shares in a single mutual fund or limited partnership account for more than 15% of your assets? If yes, score three points each for economic risk, market risk and specific risk.					
▶ Does your share in a privately held business account for more than 30% of your portfolio? If yes, score one point for economic risk and four points for specific risk.					
▶ Does a rental property account for more than 30% of your portfolio? If yes, score one point for economic risk and three points for specific risk.					
▶ Do foreign stocks and shares of domestic companies with significant overseas sales account for less than 10% of your portfolio? If yes, score one point for economic risk.					
▶ Will you need access in the next three to five years to principal in volatile assets such as stocks or long-term bonds? If yes, score one point each for inflation, interest-rate, economic and market risk.					
▶ Do you have variable-rate loans such as mortgages or credit-card revolving debt that recently has amounted to 30% or more of the market value of your portfolio? If yes, score four points for interest-rate risk.					
▶ Is 20% or more of your portfolio financed by loans or invested in highly leveraged assets such as options? If yes, score one point each for interest-rate and market risk.					
TOTAL					

manufacturers and service companies can pass along cost increases to customers relatively easily, they are more likely to prosper during periods of high inflation.

Slowing economic growth hurts some firms more than others. Manufacturers with high overhead, known as cyclicals, cannot easily cut costs when a recession slices sales, so their earnings quickly tail off. Many small growth companies also require an expanding economy to sustain their earnings growth and stock prices. By contrast, firms that sell necessities such as food or clothing often shine even in a lackluster economy, and their shares tend to hold up relatively well. Since overseas stocks are partly immune to changes in the American economy and markets, they may stand firm while U.S. stocks sink. Unlike domestic issues, however, foreign shares carry currency risk. A weaker dollar abroad helps to inflate returns that are earned on overseas assets, while a stronger dollar deflates them.

Bonds and bond funds.
Their prices fall when interest rates rise. But the extent of the drop depends on a bond's maturity and the amount of its coupon. Short-term bonds fall slightly when interest rates move upward, and a high coupon also offers some protection against climbing rates. At the opposite extreme, zero-coupon bonds fall sharply when rates head higher. A recession generally brings lower interest rates, which boost bond prices. But some issues react negatively to the threat of an economic slowdown. So-called junk bonds, in particular, may lose ground because investors fear that financially weak firms will default and fail to make payments of interest and principal to bondholders on time. U.S. Treasury and high-grade corporate bonds gain the most during hard times because income investors seek them out as safe havens.

Real estate investments.
Although they tend to keep pace with inflation over time, they present other hazards. For example, if you own a rental property, you run the risk that you won't find a tenant. A real estate

partnership that owns several properties in different regions can reduce such risks through diversification, but it may lose value if tax changes or a recession drive down property values across the country. Real estate investment trusts, called REITs, and the funds that own them, can fluctuate with the stock market as well as with property values.

Gold and other hard assets. The price of gold can skyrocket when inflation rises rapidly. Between 1968 and 1988, the consumer price index posted nine annual spurts of 6% or more. During those years, gold rewarded investors with an average gain of 34%. Gold-mining stocks are more volatile than the metal itself and expose investors to other risks. A miners' strike might boost the price of bullion but cut profits at mining companies. Other tangibles present their own problems. While antiques or rare stamps may outpace inflation in the long run, prices of items such as baseball cards are largely subject to collectors' whims.

▶ *Achieve the Best Blend for You*

Why does asset allocation determine most of an investor's return? According to researchers, the basic reason is that different types of investments don't rise and fall at the same time. By diversifying among stocks, bonds or cash, you can usually offset losses in one asset category with gains in another. For example, in October 1987, when stocks plummeted nearly 22%, long-term bonds rose 6%. The opposite proved true in 1994. Bonds tumbled 3%, while the S&P 500 eked out a 1% gain. While diversification can't guarantee that you'll never lose money, it can reduce your portfolio's overall risk and dramatically improve your odds of reaching your investment goals.

To determine the most efficient mix of investments for a retirement portfolio, experts first look at the correlation between various asset classes. Correlation is the technical term for comparing how different assets perform relative to one another over varying market cycles. The analysts measure correlation on a scale of 1.0 (two assets move precisely in tandem over time) to -1.0 (the investments always move in opposite directions). You ideally want to build a portfolio of assets that are not closely correlated to one another. That way, you won't get clobbered by all your investments dropping in value at approximately the same time.

What's more, a properly diversified portfolio lets you put some of your money in potentially high-paying assets that otherwise might be too risky. You perform this alchemy by combining them with investments to which the high fliers are only weakly correlated. For example, a portfolio entirely invested in the large domestic stocks that make up the S&P 500 would have gained over 14% a year during the past two decades. But you could have earned 16% a year over the same time with a portfolio invested 65% in S&P 500 stocks, 20% in overseas stocks (with a 0.5 correlation to U.S. blue chips) and 15% in small-company shares (a 0.8 correlation to the S&P 500). In allocating assets, the pros rely not only on stocks' and bonds' past performance but also on estimates of their potential future returns. These predictions are based on forecasts of how market cycles will affect the performance of different asset classes. The model portfolios in this chapter are based on projections that over the next 10 years or so large-company stocks will climb an average of 12% annually, bonds will rise 5% a year and cash investments such as Treasury bills will edge up almost 4% annually.

The ideal mix for life's stages. As you grow older, start a family and move closer to retirement, your investment goals and taste for risk change. Your portfolio should change along with you. Younger people, for example, can afford to aim for high returns with aggressive portfolios because they have many years to recover from market slumps. But as you get closer to retirement, you need to shift to a more cautious allocation that will preserve your gains. There's a second, equally powerful argument in favor of asset allocation. Academic studies show that about 90% of investors' returns come from the right combination of assets, with the remainder derived from their skill in picking securities and from timely trading. To help you design your own allocation, MONEY surveyed many experts to devise a model portfolio for each of the four major stages in most people's working lives—starting out, building a family, peak earning years and nearing retirement (depicted on pages 58 to 61). Of course, the portfolios described here are only rough guidelines. You should customize your allocations to meet special needs.

Aiming high in your 20s to early 30s. At this freewheeling stage, you have about 30 years before early retirement. So you can afford to gun for growth by stashing at least 80% of your portfolio in stocks and stock funds. Go for as much as 100% if you feel comfortable riding out market swings. Those who tend to get queasy in roller-coaster markets might put as much as 20% of their money in bonds and bond funds, which pay interest income that will help stabilize their portfolios. Based on past performance, this 80-20 lineup has the potential to return over 9% annually.

For beginners with small savings, a single fund that buys large-company stocks is a sound choice. Blue chips tend to offer solid capital appreciation with less volatility than smaller stocks. Nervous investors might want to opt for a balanced or asset-allocation fund instead. These all-in-one portfolios typically keep about 60% of their assets in stocks and the rest in risk-cushioning bonds and other fixed-income investments. Investors who have $10,000 or more ought to assemble a diversified portfolio of funds. Allocate about 35% of your assets to large-company stocks, 25% to small-company stocks (those with annual revenues of $500 million or less) and 20% to overseas stocks. Small stocks historically have outpaced their bigger brothers, though with greater volatility. Overseas stocks can spice up your portfolio because many foreign

Retirement Portfolios for Life's Stages

▶ Starting Out

Single Woman, Age 25 - Investment: $10,000

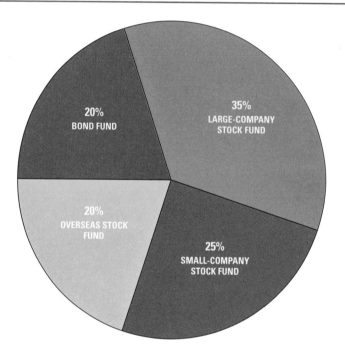

With a long way to go before retirement, she can take the necessary risks to gun for high returns. Three stock funds diversified among large and small U.S. companies plus foreign shares do that work, while a single bond fund helps to hedge her against a declining stock market. Four funds are a maximum. Any more would stretch her limited resources too much.

economies, particularly developing ones in Asia and Latin America, are likely to grow much faster than ours over the next decade. The risks you face are political instability and adverse swings in the value of the dollar. But if you can hold on through the downturns, your retirement fund could benefit greatly in the long run.

▶ Building a Family
Married Couple, Mid-Thirties, Two Preschoolers - Investment: $50,000

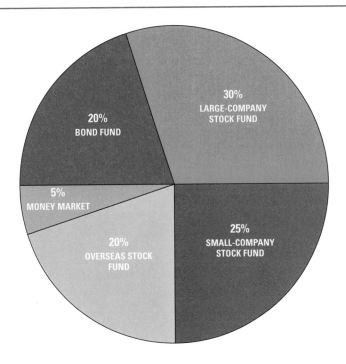

The children's eventual college bills add one more long-term expense to this young family's financial picture, making high returns a must. Thus 75% of their assets should go into stock funds, including a 25% slice in small-company funds. Depending on the couple's federal tax bracket, up to half of their bond investment should be in tax-free municipal bond funds.

For a smoother ride to those higher returns, you might include both value and growth-stock funds in your portfolio. Value managers look for out-of-favor companies with share prices that do not fully reflect their earnings prospects or asset values. By contrast, growth-stock managers, as the name suggests, prefer

Retirement Portfolios for Life's Stages

▶ Peak Earning

Married Couple, Early Fifties, Three Teenagers - Investment: $250,000

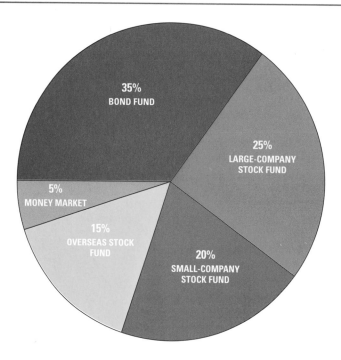

35%
BOND FUND

25%
LARGE-COMPANY
STOCK FUND

5%
MONEY MARKET

15%
OVERSEAS STOCK
FUND

20%
SMALL-COMPANY
STOCK FUND

We assume that about 60% of this couple's portfolio is already earmarked for their retirement. That portion should go entirely into U.S. and overseas stock funds that are invested for long-term capital growth. Most of the remaining money should be stashed in relatively stable, income-generating bond funds to pay for their kids' current and coming college bills.

companies with rapidly accelerating revenues and earnings, even though their shares typically will command premium prices. You can't really predict which investing style will be more successful in any given year. Studies show that over periods of 20 years or more, however, value has a slight performance advantage over growth.

about 25%, small caps to 20% and overseas stocks to 15%. This model aims to provide you with average returns of around 8% annually. You can add greater stability to your portfolio by emphasizing value funds. Since value funds focus on bargain-priced companies, they tend to fall less far than their high-flying growth peers during market corrections. And the stocks in value funds tend to pay dividends that will bolster your returns in down years. In the fixed-income portion of your portfolio, you might seek additional security by cutting international bonds to 5% and exchanging your intermediate-term corporate bond fund for one that holds government issues. Investors in the 28% bracket or above, however, will probably do better with tax-exempt bonds. To earn high returns with minimum risk, look for muni funds with annual fees of less than 1% that hold mainly bonds rated A or higher.

Kicking back in your early 50s to 60s. With retirement around the corner, you may be tempted to cash in your stock funds and tuck the proceeds into principal-preserving bond funds or bank CDs. That could prove to be a bad move. At 50 you still have a lifetime of at least 30 years ahead of you. If inflation stays at 3% a year, that will cut the purchasing power of today's dollar in half in only 12 years. Thus you should still hold a roughly 50% stake in stocks. Such a model portfolio should produce average returns of around 7.5% a year. In addition, now is an excellent time to move out of international bonds entirely and into U.S. Government issues for greater safety. Truly risk-averse investors might anchor their portfolios with Treasury notes, which mature in two to 10 years, because their principal and interest payments are federally guaranteed. You can opt for a Treasury-only bond fund. But odds are you can do just as well purchasing the Treasuries directly from the Federal Reserve Bank with no fee. For more information on how to get started, see "Be Your Own Broker With Treasury Direct" on page 64. We think that's a good deal for investors in any stage of life.

Be Your Own Broker With Treasury Direct

You can buy U.S. Treasury securities from a stockbroker or bank for commissions ranging from around $30 to $50, depending on the amount of securities that you purchase. Or you can buy them directly from the Feds and pay no fee at all. Here's what you need to know.

▶ **Bills** (minimum $10,000; recently yielding 6% to 6.6%, depending on maturity of three, six or 12 months). T-bills don't pay interest. Instead, you buy them at a discount to the face value that you will receive at maturity. The Treasury sells three- and six-month bills weekly and 12-month bills every four weeks.

▶ **Notes** (minimum $1,000 for maturities of five years or more, $5,000 for those maturing in two to five years; recently yielding 7% to 7.5%, depending on the notes' maturity). T-notes pay interest every six months. Two- and five-year notes are sold at the end of each month. Three- and 10-year notes are sold quarterly.

▶ **Bonds** (minimum $1,000; recently 7.5%). T-bonds are sold every quarter, mature in 30 years and pay interest every six months.

▶ **How to buy.** Call your nearest Federal Reserve bank or branch, listed in your phone book. Ask for the Treasury Direct package, a 10-page general information pamphlet. Fill out the package's application form and return it to the bank with a check (a certified one if you're buying T-bills). Your letter must be postmarked by midnight the day before the sale (the dates are listed in the Treasury Direct package) or your application and check will be held until the next one. Soon after the sale, the Fed will send you a letter confirming your purchase. But you won't receive bond certificates. Instead, your securities will be held in Treasury Direct's computerized records, a system known as book-entry.

▶ **Receiving interest.** The Federal Reserve will deposit your interest and, after the securities mature, your principal in your bank account. You won't know what your securities will pay you in interest every six months until after you've bought them. But you can get an estimate in advance from a broker or the *Wall Street Journal's* daily table of Treasuries traded in the resale market.

▶ **How to sell.** If you need to cash in your securities before maturity, ask the nearest Federal Reserve bank or branch for a form called a Security Transfer Request. Fill it out, return it and the bank will transfer your securities to the commercial book-entry system that banks and brokers use. Then you can sell your Treasuries via your agent for a $30 to $50 commission, of course.

▶ *Reduce Risk With These Techniques*

Are you sitting on the sidelines because the stock market looks too scary? Or waiting for prices to pull back a bit before moving more of your retirement money into stock funds? Either way, you are very likely to be disappointed. No one really knows when stock prices have no place to go but up. As a result, you may miss the chance to make some big profits. Thus investing experts often suggest that you use a risk-reducing technique for moving money into stocks and stock funds that will let you take full advantage of price dips, prevent you from getting badly hurt by sudden spikes and help assure that you reach your financial goals. The strategy, called periodic investing, has you invest regularly (e.g., every month or quarter) no matter what's happening in the market. Here are variations of this disciplined approach to investing that rely mainly on stock funds.

Dollar cost averaging. With this most basic form of periodic investing, you put a set amount each month (say, $200) in a stock fund. When stock prices fall, your $200 buys more fund shares. When prices rise, your money buys fewer. That way, you keep your shares' average cost relatively low. As shown in the table "Profit from the Installment Plan" on page 67, if you had invested $200 a month 10 years ago in Vanguard Index 500 Fund, which mimics the S&P 500 index, your $24,000 would have more than doubled to approximately $49,400. You can also try to boost your profits with a more advanced version, called progressive dollar cost averaging. This strategy takes into account inflation, the chief drawback of investing the same amount every month for years. With progressive averaging, you can increase your monthly contribution every year, or even every six months, by a set percentage. How much? Experts often recommend a manageable 10%. That will keep you far ahead of inflation as well as supercharge your savings. So an investor who starts out contributing

$200 a month might step that up to $220 a year later on. If you had used this technique over the past 10 years, your $37,950 total investment in the Vanguard Index 500 Fund would have grown to $69,800.

Value averaging. Think of this as dollar cost averaging with attitude. Rather than investing a set monthly amount, you put in whatever is necessary to hit your goal. Let's say that you need $9,000 in three years for a down payment on a house. You first open a fund account with, perhaps, $200. Next, with the help of a financial calculator or compound interest tables found in your local library's reference section, you determine that your account's value must increase $200 a month to reach your target. The actual amount you invest each month will change as stock prices fluctuate. For example, if the market is flat during the month you open your fund account, you simply invest an additional $200 in the second month, bringing your account's value to $400. On the other hand, if your fund's value falls by 12.5% during the second month, your account will dip to $350. Your third investment must then be $250, since your game plan calls for your account to be worth $600 in month three. If, however, stocks rise in the second month and boost your balance to $470, your third contribution must be only $130.

What happens if the value of your holdings rises so rapidly that your account's value exceeds your monthly target? In that case, value averaging calls for you to sell some shares. If your account increased to $700 in the third month, you would dump $100 of your holdings. Of course, your profit would be taxable if you were investing outside of a tax-deferred account, such as an IRA or 401(k) plan. Therefore, you might prefer a modified value averaging strategy called no-sell value averaging. With this technique, when your portfolio value exceeds the target, you simply do nothing that month.

Value averaging beats dollar cost averaging most of the time. To accumulate $49,400 in the index fund using our example, you would have had to invest $24,000 10 years

Profit from the Installment Plan

If you had used the value averaging method over the past 10 years, you would have earned annual returns of 15%, far more than with any of the other risk-cutting strategies shown below and explained in this chapter. In today's skittish market, however, investing experts say the three other techniques may carry less risk. In our table, we assumed that a hypothetical investor had an account with the Vanguard Index 500 Fund, which closely mimics the S&P 500 index. In the case of two related strategies, constant ratio planning and variable installment, we linked the Index 500 Fund with the Vanguard Money Market Reserves Prime Fund.

STRATEGY	MONTHLY CONTRIBUTION	TOTAL AMT. INVESTED	PORTFOLIO VALUE	AVERAGE ANNUAL RETURN	AVG. COST PER SHARE
Value averaging	Varies	$23,540	$49,400	15.1%	$20.90
Dollar cost averaging	$200	24,000	49,400	13.8	21.30
Constant ratio planning	200	24,000	40,400	9.9	28.00
Variable installment	200	24,000	40,300	9.9	29.30

ago if you used dollar cost averaging but $23,540 with value averaging. That $460 saving may seem slim. Still, your money would have worked more efficiently, delivering both higher returns and a lower average cost per share.

Constant ratio planning. This fairly conservative method calls for you to balance a stock fund investment against a less aggressive one, usually a money-market fund. You first decide how much risk you can take, then allocate your monthly investment between the two funds accordingly. Let's say you decide to split a $200 monthly investment evenly between a stock fund and a money fund. If stock prices rise, you eventually will have to shift money from your stock fund to your money fund to restore your fifty-fifty ratio. Investing experts recommend that you rebalance your portfolio whenever the ratio gets five percentage points out of whack (in our example, whenever the value of either fund rises to 55% of your portfolio). When stocks are rising, the more risk you're willing to take when you set the ratio, the more money you will make. In our example, a $200 monthly investment divided equally between the Vanguard Index 500 Fund and the Vanguard Money Market Reserves Prime Fund would have grown to $40,400, about $9,000 less than with straight dollar averaging. But you would cut your risk roughly in half by stashing 50% of your cash in a money fund.

Variable installment strategy. Like constant ratio, you start out by dividing your monthly investment equally between the funds. Then, when one fund lags the other, you direct your entire contribution to it. That way, you buy more shares when they are cheap and avoid putting money in investment categories that may be temporarily overvalued. Let's again assume you decide to invest $200 a month in a stock and a money fund. You start out by putting $100 into each. Whenever the stock fund's share price drops by an amount (let's say, 5%) that you have determined in advance, you put all of your next monthly investment into that fund. If its price rises 5%, you invest all your next monthly installment in the money fund. If you had invested a total of $24,000 10 years ago using this 5% variable installment method, your portfolio would have grown to $40,300. Like constant ratio, variable installment would have earned you about $9,000 less than straight dollar cost averaging but would have carried less risk.

▶ *Make Your Broker Work for You*

It's not exactly news that stockbrokers sometimes put their own financial interests ahead of clients' needs. Just ask an investor who was sold a rotten limited partnership in the early 1980s. So why do brokers do it? The answer is simple. Their companies often encourage them, according to a recent SEC report prepared by a five-member panel of brokerage industry experts, including Merrill Lynch chairman Daniel Tully and Berkshire Hathaway CEO Warren Buffett. The chief conclusion was that the industry's nearly universal reliance on commissions and other sales incentives inevitably leads to conflicts of interest that can hurt investors. While the report stopped short of suggesting drastic reforms, such as tying brokers' pay to their customers' investment performance, it urged firms to consider dropping widespread practices that often lead brokers to put their own interests ahead of clients'. Here are problems to be vigilant about.

Paying to push in-house funds. Of the largest brokerages, only Dean Witter still has a corporate policy of giving brokers a fatter payout for house-brand funds, though other companies may continue the practice in their branch offices. In addition, companies that don't pay higher commissions for proprietary funds can entice brokers to sell them by offering prizes or shortening the list of competing funds they are allowed to peddle. And many companies continue to pay salesmen more when they sell individual stocks and bonds from the firm's own inventory, which is more profitable than reselling securities purchased from other investors.

Running sales contests. Rewarding successful salesmen with gifts or vacations has long been a popular way to spur brokers. But the industry is beginning to acknowledge that contests based on specific products can lead brokers to push those investments on clients who aren't suited for them. The National Association of Securities Dealers, the industry group that polices brokers under the authority of the SEC, has proposed to limit such contests. Six of the seven largest brokerage houses have already dropped product-specific competitions. But all seven still award prizes to brokers for overall sales production, say,

Watch for These Investing Pitfalls

Once you have identified the various risks that reside in your retirement portfolio, you can adjust your holdings to suit your particular investment goals and temperament. That might mean, for example, reducing your interest-rate risk by lightening up your large holdings of long-term bonds. Then again, you may decide to shoulder new risks in pursuit of higher returns over time. Even the most seasoned and market-savvy investors frequently make mistakes. What follows, however, are some common investment errors that you should try to avoid.

▶ **Having too much money in your company's stock.** Investors who concentrate a sizable share of their assets in any single stock are courting trouble. Many make the mistake, often without even knowing it, because they invest heavily in the shares of the corporation they work for through vehicles such as 401(k) and profit-sharing plans.

▶ **Leaving too much money in cash.** Some investors escape the perils of stock market volatility, bond defaults and real estate slumps by keeping the bulk of their assets in cash. But they often overlook the even more relentless threat of inflation. Cash equivalents such as Treasury bills, short-term bonds and money-market funds carry almost no risk—and no chance for capital gains that can outpace rising prices.

▶ **Assembling a portfolio piecemeal.** You may be a genius at spotting enticingly undervalued stocks or choosing top-performing mutual funds. But a collection of great individual investments does not always provide the balance your portfolio needs. If you have already loaded up on stocks, for example, you probably should pass on that promising new stock pick you read about and buy income-generating bonds or real estate instead.

▶ **Buying more investments than you can monitor.** To diversify fully, you may be tempted to own so many assets that you do not have time to follow them all carefully. Or you may buy investments for which accurate information is hard to obtain. Remember that less can be more. Choose a mutual fund or two instead of a host of individual stocks to fill out the gaps in your diversification plan.

▶ **Overlooking important assets.** Many investors focus their diversification efforts too narrowly, excluding major assets such as their rising earning power, appreciating home and mounting tax-deferred accounts. But such assets may be the most valuable. If your 401(k) is stashed in long-term bonds and cash, for example, you should consider tilting your remaining assets toward growth-oriented investments.

or total fund commissions earned. The SEC committee warned that even these broad contests can put brokers' interests and customers' interests at odds.

Recruiting brokers with incentives. To lure brokers from rivals, many firms use both up-front bonuses and the promise of higher commissions for a period of perhaps three to six months. If a broker's clients want to follow her to the new firm, she could pressure them to replace their current funds with shares purchased through the new brokerage. That, of course, would mean a new round of sales charges for the broker. What's more, those special recruitment commissions, which can run double the normal rate, encourage excessive trading, or churning, of customers' accounts. Of the firms surveyed, only Edward D. Jones forswears recruiting bonuses, and Paine Webber has announced plans to stop paying higher commissions to recruits. "A good broker wouldn't do anything one way vs. another, but why entice anybody?" says Paine Webber president Joseph Grano. He adds that brokers switching firms should be required to disclose up-front bonuses when they ask clients to move with them.

Putting trainees on commission. Requiring novice brokers to live entirely off their commissions "creates an atmosphere in which aggressive selling and unsuitable recommendations are bound to take place," the study found. The panel recommended weaning trainees from salary to commissions gradually over a period of two to three years. None of the big seven currently keep their new brokers on salary for more than two years.

Rewarding profits, not compliance. Branch managers whose pay is based solely on their office's profits are more likely to ignore unethical practices by their staff. At Edward D. Jones, however, brokers with poor compliance may be barred from becoming limited partners in the firm, and Paine Webber fines managers whose branches fail audits. Paine Webber adds that it has instituted a new retirement plan for brokers that penalizes them for poor compliance. The panel also found that no firm excelled at revealing such basic data as the special incentives brokers receive or how customers' investments have performed.

What influence will the report have? It remains largely a wish list. The SEC has no plans to issue new rules based on the panel's conclusions. SEC chairman Arthur Levitt, who is a former broker, says he doesn't want the government mandating compensation programs. SEC chief of staff Michael Schlein, who served as liaison between the SEC and the committee, echoes his boss' theme. "We are trying to encourage firms to compete to find ways of putting clients first," he says. "We want to give them some time."

Until then, you should continue to make every effort to assure that your broker acts in your best interests. Before you invest, always ask the broker to tell you how much you'll pay in commission and fees for any product or service he recommends. Then find out whether the charges are negotiable. If the investment carries a commission of more than 5%, ask whether there's a less costly alternative. Then probe for potential conflicts of interest. Ask whether your broker stands to get any extra compensation or other reward for selling the particular product he is pushing. If so, then the burden of proof is on the broker to prove the proposal is clearly in your interest. Don't invest unless the broker convinces you that the recommended product is clearly better than alternatives that the broker has less personal reason to push.

▶ Rating the Top Brokerages' Services

Want an investment pro who can guide your retirement plan to princely profits? If so, you had better stay alert. That's the disappointing conclusion from MONEY's survey of the nation's leading full-service brokerage firms. The study was performed for us by Prophet Market Research & Consulting of San Francisco. Overall, its testers found that brokers scored a middling 76 out of a possible 100 points. Brokers got high marks in some important areas, with 92% of them providing fairly cautious investment advice. But they also offered some misinformation about risks, expenses and returns. Thus, to get the full service you expect from full-cost firms, you need to be vigilant about making sure your broker doesn't fall into the pot-holes our survey identified. Here's what we found.

Even leaders fell short of superior. An excellent score on this test would have been 85. We expected an average of 80. Yet the highest scoring firm, Edward D. Jones, finished barely above the expected average at 82. The lowest scoring firms, Sutro & Co. and Advest, ended below it by a much larger margin, with scores of 68 and 67, respectively.

Big firms treat customers better. The six large brokerages we rated outscored the 15 smaller ones by a difference of 79 to 70, on average. Yet the overall winner, the aforementioned Edward D. Jones, is at the high end of the small side, with 3,382 brokers and 3,312 offices in 50 states. And you find good and bad apples everywhere. Smith Barney, for instance, employed both the lowest ranked broker in our survey (with a 32 score) and one of the four brokers who aced the test with a perfect 100.

Brokers often don't know clients. Some 42% of brokers offered advice to our testers without ever asking about their tax bracket, an important piece of investing information. About 39% didn't inquire about their income. Brokers also tend to ignore or play down risk. About 75% of the brokers who were pitching overseas stock funds neglected to say that currencies' shifting exchange rates could torpedo the value of these funds. Nearly a third who recommended stocks neglected to say anything about commissions.

Here's how our study was conducted. Prophet sent trained testers to meet with 25 brokers at each of the six largest national firms (Merrill Lynch, Smith Barney, Dean

How Big and Small Brokers Stack Up

RANK/FIRM	NUMBER OF OFFICES/BROKERS	OVERALL SCORE (OUT OF 100)	INTERVIEW/ ADVICE SCORE* (OUT OF 5)	COMMENTS
LARGER FIRMS				
1 A.G. Edwards	510/5,400	81.6	4.0	Its brokers don't seem to have incentives favoring the firm at client's expense.
2 Dean Witter	360/8,000	80.1	3.8	Dean Witter pays its brokers extra to sell the firm's in-house investment products.
3 Merrill Lynch	500/12,500	79.5	4.0	Its brokers tend to push a $175 financial plan intended to help you meet goals.
4 Smith Barney	475/11,200	78.8	3.8	Brokerage scored best at giving clients realistic idea of expected returns.
5 Paine Webber	328/6,400	76.5	3.5	Only 42% of its brokers gave clients prospectuses, the least of a large firm.
6 Prudential	270/5,650	75.6	3.5	Prudential is finally abandoning higher payouts for selling in-house funds.
SMALLER FIRMS				
1 Edward D. Jones	3,312/3,382	81.9	3.9	Most brokers run their own offices. The firm does not sell in-house funds.
2 Raymond James	41/450	80.9	3.8	This brokerage offers clients detailed confirmation reports with cost and risks.
3 Kemper Securities	150/1,200	80.1	3.8	Its brokers scored the best of any firm at explaining mutual funds.
4 J.C. Bradford	76/725	79.9	3.7	Though known as a bond house, half of Bradford's sales are stocks.
5 Legg Mason	90/900	78.9	3.6	Its funds have loads but no front- or back-end charges.
6 Alex. Brown	19/434	77.3	3.4	This firm does not pay brokers extra for selling in-house funds.
7 Dain Bosworth	67/854	75.3	3.3	Some 86% of its brokers offered fund prospectus, second highest of all firms.
8 Robert W. Baird	284/3,5981	75.3	3.7	Baird came in with the lowest score for explaining investment products clearly.
9 Piper Jaffray	76/1,015	75.2	3.5	Lowest proportion of brokers (only 40%) said past gains don't predict future.
10 Tucker Anthony	31/440	72.8	3.3	Brokers at Tucker scored the best of any firm on overall product knowledge.
11 Janney Montgomery	42/625	71.9	3.2	Janney tied for the worst at asking about their clients' investment history.
12 Gruntal	31/800	71.0	3.1	Brokerage tied for lowest score on telling clients to keep cash reserve.
13 Fahnestock	47/490	70.0	3.0	Two of Fahnestock's brokers pitched highly speculative stock ideas.
14 Sutro	15/246	68.4	3.0	This firm tied Gruntal for the lowest score on assessing customer assets.
15 Advest	90/530	67.0	3.3	Brokerage scored lowest of any firm surveyed on overall customer service.

* Includes factors related to quality of advice and how well broker interviewed subject to determine his or her needs, assets, risk tolerance and the like.

Witter Reynolds, Paine Webber, Prudential Securities and A.G. Edwards & Sons) and with 10 brokers apiece from 15 smaller, mostly regional brokerages. The testers posed as novice investors with roughly $40,000 that they wanted to invest safely. After the meetings, which lasted about one hour each, they graded the brokers on specific measurements of service, advice and compliance with investment law. Prophet then combined weighted test results to compute an overall score for each firm. Some firms complained that our samples of 10 and 25 brokers were simply too small. Just by luck of the draw, they said, we may have happened on 10 clunkers at one company and 10 stars at the next. That's certainly possible. But it doesn't excuse the misinformation and poor service the testers received from the fully employed clunkers. Even if you leave aside the individual results (which we believe would be a mistake), you are forced to conclude that brokerages could do a far better job of training and policing their troops. Here's advice gleaned from the survey.

Insist brokers learn more about you. When you go to a full-service broker, you want advice that's tailored to you. But all too often the advisers that we consulted based their recommendations on scant knowledge of their customers. Besides skipping over some questions about income and tax bracket, many salesmen didn't even determine the client's time horizon, a key measure of how much risk an investor can tolerate. Several firms excused these oversights by saying that brokers don't bear down on sensitive topics until a customer opens an account. Nevertheless, industry rules require that salesmen know customers before giving advice. No recommendations should be made until the broker has sufficient information about a person, including income, tax bracket and level of sophistication. One Smith Barney salesman suggested that the tester put 40% of his portfolio in overseas stock funds without knowing his income, his wife's income, their federal tax bracket or whether they had any retirement savings. Wrote the tester: "The fact that he had most of the plan done before I arrived at the meeting, when he knew virtually nothing of my story, is scary." By comparison, nine of 10 Kemper brokers asked clients about their tax bracket, and 90% of Raymond James and Merrill Lynch salespeople completed a written financial profile of their clients.

Demand data on risks and returns. Virtually every broker who recommended stocks discussed the chance of stock market losses. But their candor dropped off sharply when it came to other investments, notably bond funds. Nearly a quarter of advisers peddling such funds did a poor job of explaining interest-rate risk. At A.G. Edwards, for example, one salesman explained that government bonds are considered safer than bank CDs because they are direct obligations of the government. That's true if the bonds are held to maturity. But the broker failed to disclose that even government issues can lose value if rates rise. Bear market performance was sometimes swept aside too. One Prudential broker showed our tester a typewritten sheet highlighting a fund's strong gains over the previous year. But when the client asked to see how the fund fared in down markets, the broker said it only was possible to look at results for entire years. Yet rating services calculate returns weekly or monthly for virtually all funds.

Watch out for proprietary pitches. When your broker makes a recommendation, it should fit your investment profile and not just pad his paycheck. But some firms use incentives like higher commissions to encourage brokers to sell in-house products that earn the firm higher profits. The worst offender in this regard was Dean Witter. Two-thirds of its brokers surveyed by our testers suggested at least one proprietary product. That may be because the firm pays brokers two to five percentage points more for selling an in-house fund than an independent company's comparable offering. But what's good for Dean Witter isn't necessarily best for you. Other firms that routinely promoted their own investments included Merrill Lynch and Smith Barney.

4

Smart Moves For Today's Markets

*I*n June 1994, when stocks were slumping and many investors were gripped by gloom, MONEY's cover story "Buy Stocks Now!" said: "Forget today's frightening headlines. And ignore tomorrow's choppy stock prices. We are on track for one of the great stock-buying opportunities of a lifetime." We went on to lay out our case for higher share prices. Individuals clearly favor investing in mutual funds over saving in bank accounts. The country's restructured companies are again the most competitive in the world. As a result, corporate profits are set to grow 8% to 9% a year, on average. Yet stock valuations remain reasonable. Therefore, we concluded that the Dow figured to surpass 5,000 before the decade ends. With the Dow recently above 4,600, up more than 20% from its June 1994 low, our predictions no longer seem so radical.

MONEY's stock market forecast. Now we see the Dow going on to top 5,000 perhaps as early as 1999. All in all, that's a happy prospect for investors in stocks and stock funds. Counting dividends, you can earn an average of about 8% annually in blue chips over the next five years. With smart selections, you could achieve double-digit returns. The catch is that within the next two years the stock market could temporarily drop 15%. We don't think that decline will begin in 1995. With inflation still low and corporations reporting record profits, the stock market seems to be on solid ground. Moreover, Alan Greenspan is up for reappointment as Federal Reserve chairman in March 1996 and wants to maintain today's

Goldilocks economy—not too hot, not too cold, just right. But he'll have to keep fine-tuning interest rates to achieve it. (See our interest-rate outlook below.)

If the economy were to strengthen, a big surge in inflation would catch investors by surprise. It's conventional wisdom that inflation is belly up in the water at just over 3%. Nonetheless, average raw materials prices have risen 15% to 20% in the past year. Those increases, in turn, have helped drive up the prices of industrial materials by about 7%. Unless the economy continues to slow, some of those price hikes could spread to the retail level. And that could scare investors into dumping stocks. On the other hand, if the economy were to weaken, corporate profits could disappoint investors. So far, shareholders are understandably delighted with corporate earnings. Profits are running 22% ahead of the year-ago figures and about 5% above what analysts expected. If the economy stalls entirely, however, profits could upset investors by lagging expectations.

What events would signal that the economy is too hot? We wouldn't want to see monthly inflation of 0.4% or more and interest-rate increases greater than half a point (short-term rates at 6.5% and long-term rates at 7.8%). What would be a sign that the economy is too cold? We would get a chill from a falloff in job growth to only 100,000 a month, down from 236,000 lately. More likely, Greenspan will stay lucky and the economy will remain just right for a while. As long as you're prepared to ride out temporary stock market downturns, your blue chips and stock funds stand an excellent chance of earning an average of 8% to 10% annually through the rest of the decade.

MONEY's bond market forecast. Whether or not Congress ever passes a balanced budget amendent, our legislators are going to cut the federal deficit and entitlements (Medicare, Medicaid, Social Security, veterans' benefits and the like). They have no choice, really. They have already run through the easy reductions, such as assaulting the military budget. The Bush and Clinton

Administrations shrank discretionary spending from 9.7% of the total economy in 1988 to 7.7% recently. But that wasn't enough. The deficit remains stuck at around $200 billion because entitlements have swelled from 10.3% to 12%. If they keep growing, by 2005 they could eat up another two percentage points of the economy, or an additional $200 billion a year.

We don't think that will happen. Now that more than 70% of the voters say they want the deficit cut, political pressure is intensifying. Before long, the government will have to start whittling down entitlements. Letting the deficit keep growing would be even more painful, leading to inflation, soaring interest rates and a collapsing dollar. The bottom line? Once investors see entitlements get the ax, they'll acknowledge that serious deficit reduction is under way by helping trigger a long-term decline in interest rates. Bonds and bond funds figure to boom along with other income investments such as electric utilities. The trend to lower rates will be helped by moderate inflation. Labor costs, which account for two-thirds of long-term inflation pressure, are rising a modest 3% a year. Although other costs may push inflation to as high as 3.5% to 4% in the next two years, we think it will peak there. Once the next recession hits, long-term interest rates will likely drop through the 5.8% low we saw in October 1993.

If we're right, bonds and bond funds are terrific buys. If yields on 30-year Treasuries drop from today's 6.6% to 5.5% within the next five years, holders would enjoy solid capital gains as well as steady income. If a temporary rise in inflation pushes yields above 8%, the subsequent fall to 5.5% in five years would mean an annual return of about 12%. So consider any significant decline in bond prices as a buying opportunity. A similar case can be made for electric utilities and other income stocks (those with dividend yields above 4%).

Forget about market timing. No one can consistently jump in and out of the stock and bond markets, nimbly pocketing profits and avoiding losses as prices rise and fall. Consider this hypothetical example. Two investors each put $10,000 into a typical growth stock fund just before the October 1987 market crash. The first panics at the market plunge and sells out, losing 27%, and sticks the remaining $7,300 into a money-market fund yielding 5%. In 1990, he moves back into a growth fund to catch the market's rise, only to bolt to a money fund again nine months later after the growth fund tumbles 11%. The second investor, meanwhile, sits tight in the growth fund the entire time. When they compare the value of their accounts recently, who do you suppose fared better? For all his moves in and out, the panicky investor has only $8,900 left. That's a nearly 11% loss. By comparison, the buy-and-hold investor's account grew 84% to $18,400. And the sooner you begin investing, the better off you will be. So get going.

▶ Double Your Savings in Five Years

If you're just beginning to learn the ways of Wall Street, you aren't yet in a position to take risks with your retirement money. If you're an established investor with a well-diversified nest egg, however, you may want to consider some of the potential winners evaluated here. Your ambitious goal is to double your money in five years. If this seems unrealistic, like winning the lottery, keep in mind that all you need to succeed is an annual return of 15%. True, that's about 1.5 times the 10% annual long-term return of the S&P 500 stocks. Yet, in the five years since Standard & Poor's started tracking such numbers, 147 of those stocks would have doubled your money with dividends reinvested. Below are 10 diverse investments that as a group could achieve that total return in five years.

Go for growth in earnings. With U.S. economic growth cooling to an estimated 2.5% a year, companies that can post dependable double-digit earnings gains will outperform the pack. In this category, we zero in on an aggressive stock fund targeting high-growth small companies. And we feature two stock picks from Dallas money manager Susan Byrne. Her Westwood Equity Fund has chalked up a 9% annual gain over the past three years, vs. 7% for stock funds as a group.

▶ **Boeing.** Its business tends to move in cycles of five to six years based on world airlines' need to upgrade their fleets. The $22 billion (annual sales) Seattle plane maker now seems poised for a steep ascent. Byrne expects Boeing to snag about half of the 6,700 new aircraft orders she projects over the next five years (vs. 3,000 over the past five). Propitious signs abound. Boeing, which gets 57% of its revenues from foreign customers, has won the bidding for 35 new 737 jetliners from the Scandinavian Airlines System (SAS). And it has begun delivering its new 777 generation of planes, which analysts estimate will attract 200 orders a year. Moreover, Boeing will be building its planes with fewer employees after laying off an estimated 7,000 of its 123,000 workers in 1995.

▶ **Lockheed Martin.** With the Pentagon budget down 9% over the past three years, stocks of military contractors have been strafed. But the merger of Lockheed and Martin Marietta has created a $23 billion firm that seems likely to lead the market, grabbing 15% of the estimated $400 billion in new government contracts awarded over the next five years. Moreover, Lockheed Martin (based in Bethesda, Md.) plans to slash operating costs by $2 billion to $3 billion over the next five years. The combination of sales growth and cost cutting, Byrne estimates, will inflate earnings an average of 15% a year, enough for a double even without any improvement in its depressed PE (price-earnings) ratio of 9. "Even if people hate defense stocks in the future as much as they do today, which may well not be true, we could get the double," she says. In addition, Lockheed Martin will enjoy $800 million in free cash flow that Byrne anticipates will be put toward paying a dividend and buying back company stock, helping to boost the share price.

▶ **Wasatch Aggressive Equity.** As a group, small stocks have outperformed their bigger brethren, returning 12% annually over time relative to 10% for the large-company stocks in the S&P 500. But trolling for small fish is tricky. Research tends to be spotty and the risks of landing a loser are high. So for small-cap stocks, we recommend sticking with mutual funds. In our screening, Wasatch Aggressive Equity emerged with one of the highest portfolio earnings growth rates (27%) among all funds whose holdings had a median market value of less than $300 million. Boasting an average annual return of nearly 17%, Wasatch more than doubled shareholders' money over the past five years and shows no signs of flagging. The fund's four-member management team aims for a measure of stability by keeping half the assets of the portfolio in mid-size, dependable growth companies. The other half goes into high-flying "emerging growth" firms, sometimes with revenues of less than $25 million. "We are buying companies so small that there are no or very few analysts following them," says lead manager Sam Stewart, who has headed the fund since its 1986 inception. "Thus we hope to get a big price boost when other analysts and investors get interested later."

Aim for a double via dividends. Steady dividend growth can give a similar booster shot to stocks. After all, investors bid up share prices in expectation of future returns, whether those returns come as income or capital gains. To spot companies strong enough to pump up their profits as well as their payouts, we consulted lead manager John Snyder of John Hancock Sovereign Investors Fund, which considers only stocks of companies that have raised dividends for 10 straight years. We then supplemented his two dynamic dividend favorites with an electric utility other pros tout as a possible two bagger.

▶ **Alco Standard.** As the nation's largest independent distributor of business machines and paper for office and other uses, $8 billion Alco is riding the booming demand for fax machines and color copiers. Snyder sees earnings growing at least 16% a year over the next five years and projects annual dividend growth of about 13%. "This company generates tremendous cash flow, and it will pass some of it along to shareholders," he predicts. Alco recently was selling at some 20 times its estimated annual earnings, compared with about 15 for the S&P 500. But its projected earnings and dividend growth are both at least double those of the index.

▶ **Abbott Laboratories.** Among pharmaceutical stocks, Snyder believes $9 billion Abbott remains undervalued in relation to its prospective earnings and dividend growth. In addition to new asthma and ulcer drugs, Abbott is bringing out new cost-efficient diagnostic equipment for hospitals and laboratories. Snyder and other analysts project Abbott's earnings growth at 13% a year over the next five years. Dividends should climb 12% annually. That combination should produce a double even if investors do not boost the PE ratio above the recent 17 level.

▶ **CMS Energy.** Utility analyst Barry Abramson of Prudential Securities believes $3.6 billion CMS, which supplies electricity and gas to southern Michigan outside Detroit, is a strong candidate to thrive in the increasingly competitive environment for utilities. CMS has a subsidiary that explores for oil and natural gas and markets the gas. The unit also invests in power plants in fast-growing countries such as India, the Philippines and Argentina. Such operations represent only 7% of revenues now. "But significant earnings growth from the nonutility side of the business gives CMS an exceptional earnings outlook," says Abramson. He predicts that a combination of 5% yearly earnings growth plus dividend growth of 12% annually are destined to produce a double in five years.

Bet on a Brady Bunch rebound. Emerging markets have been hammered since Mexico's peso devaluation in late 1994. But many overseas veterans believe panicky investors have driven some markets down too far. Over the next three to five years, Latin and Asian

economies are projected to grow an average of 6% annually, twice the rate for developed economies. That superior performance will inevitably resuscitate many a battered market around the globe. Our choices are closed-end stock funds traded on the New York Stock Exchange. Such funds sell at prices that can be greater or less than their NAVs (net asset values), depending upon investor demand. When closed-ends sell at a discount to NAV, they have the potential to deliver double-barreled gains. Their NAVs can rise, and the discounts can narrow or turn into premiums. To further improve the odds of a double, we've selected funds that concentrate their holdings primarily on a single region or type of security. That tight focus makes them both potentially more profitable, and riskier, than broader portfolios. Our guide to the best opportunities in global closed-end funds is analyst Michael Porter of Smith Barney.

Among your best shots for scoring a double in an emerging market are so-called Brady bonds. They are issued by nations in Latin America, Eastern Europe, Asia and Africa. But they are named for former U.S. Treasury Secretary Nicholas Brady, who devised them as a way to ease the Third World's debt crisis. The bonds offer several advantages. They are denominated in dollars, and thus immune to swings in exchange rates. If the nation runs into interim economic problems, up to three semi-annual interest payments are secured with U.S. corporate bonds. Of course, there's the risk that a nation would not resume interest payments. But that's unlikely because it would cut off access to the capital these nations desperately need. Finally, the U.S. Treasury guarantees payback of principal. The payoff? Price declines of up to 18% have knocked down Brady bonds to levels that lately produced yields of 16% to 18%.

▶ **Scudder World Income.** Porter thinks this entry is the best buy among closed-end funds holding Brady bonds. It has nearly half its assets in Brazil, Argentina, Peru and Venezuela, with the balance in government and corporate debt from other emerging economies. Porter notes that manager Isabel Saltzman is a tested pro. The bonds the fund holds will gain about 10% a year in price, Porter estimates. That gain, combined with five years of the fund's recent 12% yield, would add up to a 110% profit.

▶ **G.T. Global Developing Markets.** Porter suggests this fund, run by Jim Bogin, for conservative investors who are most concerned with limiting their potential downside by buying at a big discount. Its portfolio recently mixed 39% Brady and other emerging market bonds with 55% mostly Latin American stocks. G.T. Financial Management is one of the most experienced companies in Latin markets, says Porter, who adds that the stockholdings should help the fund turn in a double when Latin markets rebound.

Profit from falling rates. With the Federal Reserve signaling that it may be done raising interest rates, long-term rates could fall to around 5.5% over the next three years. That would bring fat capital gains for bondholders. With this possibility in mind, we requested two bond picks from Richard Lehmann of the *Income Securities Advisor* newsletter.

▶ **General Motors Acceptance** (GMAC) zero-coupon bond of 2012 (recently priced around $240 per $1,000 and yielding 8.5% if held to maturity). Zero-coupon bonds pay no interest. Instead, you buy them at a discount and receive their full face value at maturity. The lack of regular payouts makes zeros far more volatile than standard bonds, which can bring trouble when rates climb but a bonanza when they fall. "If overall interest rates come down two percentage points, which we think is likely, you would get a double right there with this GMAC issue," notes Lehmann. Backed by GM auto loans, these bonds have a low risk of default. And they offer an advantage over other zeros. You normally must pay annual taxes on the interest your zero accrues each year even though you receive no cash. But the GMAC and two other zeros (another GMAC and one from an Exxon subsidiary) escape the "phantom interest" rule because they were issued in 1982 before the IRS made that regulation. Thus you pay tax only when you sell your bonds or they mature.

▶ **Greyhound Lines** 10% bonds of 2001 (recently priced at $725 per $1,000 and yielding about 13.5%). After a string of losses that brought it to the brink of bankruptcy, the nation's largest intercity bus company has installed new management and completed a financial restructuring designed to slash debt from 78% of its total capitalization to about 50%. Lehmann believes Greyhound is now healthy enough to keep up its interest payments. "As Greyhound's improved situation becomes clearer, I think these bonds will get a credit upgrade from the recent level of CCC," he predicts. "That could boost the price a third." Even without an upgrade, the normal price appreciation that occurs as a bond nears maturity would likely complete the double in five years or so. The risk is that Greyhound takes another wrong turn and fails to make all of its interest payments. But Lehmann believes that steady business from budget-conscious travelers will keep Greyhound and its bonds on the road to recovery.

▶ *Run a Reality Check on Your Funds*

Investing in mutual funds is definitely more demanding these days. Take something as basic as knowing what kinds of funds you now own. Garden variety U.S. stock funds, you say? Better check again. To juice up their returns, some of these fund managers routinely load up on volatile emerging market stocks. As for that seemingly ultrasafe short-term government bond fund you own, have you peeked in a recent quarterly report to see whether it's bristling with risky derivatives? These are complex instruments whose value is based on some underlying asset, commodity or interest-rate index. Have you added up your fund's overt and covert charges to learn how much you're really paying in expenses? Such chores didn't seem all that pressing in the 1980s and early 1990s, when even indifferently managed funds were chalking up big gains. Then came a brutal year like 1994, when many foreign stock exchanges melted down, domestic bond prices blew up and U.S. stock markets meandered. Now smart investors realize that they have to do more homework to make money.

To that end, here are some guidelines that will enable you to master the new complexities of fund investing and make the most of what is shaping up as a strong year for investors. In the first six months of 1995, the S&P 500 index returned roughly 20%, compared with only 1% in all of 1994. Moreover, despite currency crises and turmoil in emerging markets, savvy investors can still ferret out overseas funds capable of compelling returns. Indeed, as more countries move from socialism to privatization, the outlook for the global economy has improved considerably. Even the downtrodden U.S. bond market is looking up again following a series of inflation-thwarting hikes in interest rates by Federal Reserve chairman Alan Greenspan. To reap your share of these gains without repeating 1994's mistakes, start boning up on the guidelines below.

Ensure funds aren't impostors. You can't simply rely on a fund's name or investment category to tell you how its manager actually invests. No matter how innocuous-sounding the fund name, the manager may stray into alarmingly risky territory to post eye-catching returns. In 1994, income-minded investors who owned two supposedly safe short-term bond funds, Piper Jaffray Institutional Government and Paine Webber Short-Term U.S. Government, were hit with losses of 29% and 5%, respectively, because the managers had stocked up on volatile mortgage-backed derivatives.

Stock funds also can have the investing equivalent of a split personality. For example, a fund named Dean Witter American Value would seem to suggest that it pursues a value strategy when, in fact, it invests for growth.

So anyone who put money in the fund from 1992 to 1994, when value funds scored 8% annual gains, would have been disappointed by the fund's corresponding 5% return. A fund named Berger 101, ostensibly a domestic stock fund, held more than a 30% stake in 1994 in foreign stocks, which contributed greatly to its 9% loss for that year. To get a fix on how a fund actually invests, you should first read its prospectus carefully. Berger 101's prospectus lets the manager stash any amount of the fund's assets in foreign stocks. Then you should regularly monitor the fund's holdings by examining its quarterly report, which lists every security in the portfolio.

Factor in past performance. One of the biggest mistakes investors make is buying a fund just because it's topped the performance charts over a short period. Funds that climb to the top of the charts in one year often crash and burn the next. That's because blazing short-term gains tend to be fueled by big bets on a hot industry sector or investing style that is about to cool. For years financial advisers have discouraged you from buying a fund solely because of its past performance. Looking back can tell how well a manager has handled good and bad markets, they said. But it can't reveal how a fund will do in the future.

But look again. At least three recent studies claim a fund's record does shed light on future performance. In the most comprehensive survey, Yale finance professors William Goetzmann and Roger Ibbotson looked into the relationship between past and future results of 728 stock funds over four successive three-year periods starting in 1976. They compared 1976-78 returns with those in 1979-81, 1979-81 returns with those in 1982-84 and so on. The professors found that a manager who finished in the top quarter of stock funds in the initial three-year periods had a 72% chance of ranking in the top half and a 41% likelihood of making the top quarter in the subsequent three-year periods. Conversely, a fund that initially finished in the bottom quarter had only a 13% chance of climbing into the top half in the follow-up periods. Their conclusion is that managers who have outperformed their peers in the past are likely, though not guaranteed, to repeat in the future. Many advisers suggest that you look at performance over at least five years, however. That way, you can be sure the record reflects the manager's skill and not merely a lucky streak or a period that favored his specialty (say, high-tech stocks).

Watch out for onerous fees. When funds were routinely churning out double-digit returns over the 1980s, most investors didn't mind paying bloated annual expenses. But in tougher times, when even half a percentage point can represent a sizable portion of a typical fund's yearly gain or loss, it pays to make sure a fund's expense ratio doesn't exceed the category average. In the case of bond funds, high expenses may lead a manager to take on too many risks. Since few fixed-income managers can beat the averages, those saddled with high expenses are tempted to take more risk to overcome the drag of their fees. So stick with bond funds that charge no more than the average 0.9% annual expense ratio. Recent studies by the SEC and by Princeton economist Burton Malkiel make an equally strong case for favoring low-expense stock funds. Their research shows that for every percentage point the typical stock fund spends on expenses, its return falls almost two percentage points. Those higher expenses are commonly caused by frequent trading of investments, which tends to reduce returns. Since you aren't buying better performance by paying higher fees, give preference to stock funds that levy no more than the 1.5% average expense ratio.

▶ *Fallen Stars Poised for Comebacks*

After struggling in 1994's punishing markets, these distinguished funds seem poised to surge convincingly over the coming years. By buying shares in them now, you will be practicing a form of value investing—betting on out-of-favor fund managers who have the potential to rebound with market-beating gains. All appear ready to regain their star status within the next three years or so, making them excellent choices for long-term investors deploying their retirement portfolios. There's one caveat, however. Most of these funds have incurred 10% to 20% more volatility than their peers in recent years. But patient investors should be well rewarded over time for the rocky ride.

Pasadena Growth. This growth fund is up a scant 0.4% annually over the past three years, placing it in the bottom 2% of growth funds ranked by Morningstar. Nonetheless, manager Roger Engemann remains one of the best large-cap growth investors around, ferreting out companies whose earnings accelerate 15% a year or more. For example, the fund's 68% gain in 1991 nearly doubled the average growth portfolio's 37% return and placed Pasadena in the top 3% of growth funds. And the fund is up 11% for the past 12 months, compared with 9% for the average growth fund. Says Engemann: "Our train is beginning to pick up steam, and it's got at least three years of growth ahead." To keep the fund on track, he has placed 70% of his assets in large companies with near monopolies, such as $16 billion (in annual sales) Coca-Cola and $6 billion Gillette. "With their proven prowess, I feel confident they can maintain their strong growth," he says. He also has built a 5% stake in high-tech stocks, including $22 billion Motorola and $12 billion Intel. Earnings for both figure to keep bounding ahead by 20% a year or better.

Warburg Pincus International. Manager Richard King is coping with a life of extremes. Despite a meltdown in foreign markets that dealt his fund a nearly 3% loss over the past 12 months, King has had to grapple with how to invest more than $1 billion that investors poured into Warburg's coffers, presumably because of the fund's staggering 53% gain in 1993. That year was no fluke for King. His portfolio has returned 17% annually from the fund's 1989 start-up through 1993, trouncing his peers' 11% gain and the 3% advance of Morgan

Stanley's EAFE index of European, Australasian and Far Eastern stocks. King expects to regain his most favored fund status as a slowing U.S. economy entices investors into faster-growing international markets over the next year. That move should bolster foreign share prices—and profits for King's shareholders. He has plowed a third of the fund's assets into European companies like $3 billion VA Technologie, an Austrian engineering firm that he expects to profit from the development of Eastern Europe. He has also stashed 30% of the fund's money in Japanese stocks, mostly technology and manufacturing firms whose earnings could boom as Japan recovers from its recession. Another 10% is tucked away in the emerging Asian markets of Korea, Malaysia and Taiwan, plus 4% in volatile Latin America. "These countries may be bumpy short term," says King. "But they are growing at twice the rate of developed economies." Rounding out his stock portfolio are stakes in Australia and in New Zealand, which he lauds as a "terrific little economy that's got it right."

T. Rowe Price New America Growth. The fund's co-managers John Laporte and Brian Berghuis stock up on quickly growing firms in the U.S. service economy, which has expanded every year since World War II. Spurred by that growth, New America has gained 14% annually for the past five years and ranked in the top 15% of growth funds. Last year, however, the portfolio lost 7%, which put it behind 85% of its competitors. The problem? As the economy boomed, investors bid up cyclical stocks and shunned service companies' shares. But as economic growth slows, investors will turn to stocks with steady earnings, including the service firms the fund zeroes in on. That already seems to be happening. In the first quarter the fund gained 9%, compared with 8% for growth funds overall. About 44% of the fund is invested in business services, which include everything from health care to waste disposal. Another 40% or so is salted away in consumer stocks, such as $1 billion CUC International, the leading provider of direct-mail discount

shopping services. Since the company has no major competitors, Berghuis and Laporte think it can maintain its rapid earnings gains of more than 20% a year.

Fidelity Asset Manager Growth. This asset-allocation fund has been painfully out of step with competitors over the past year, falling to the bottom 8% of its category with a 2% loss. The chief culprit was a 15% stake in volatile, emerging market stocks and bonds, mostly Mexican. But manager Bob Beckwitt isn't panicking because of one year in which nearly all of his 15 or so investment allocations performed poorly. "My goal is to make money over a full market cycle," says Beckwitt. "And I've done that in the past." And how. Even counting 1994's wretched performance, the fund's nearly 11% annualized return since its start-up in 1992 puts the portfolio in the top 10% of similar funds. Beckwitt also manages the less aggressive Fidelity Asset Manager, which has gained 12% annually for the past five years, placing it in the top 4% of its category. Anticipating that the Federal Reserve might hike rates again, which would pound stock prices, Beckwitt has recently pared his usual 65% stock allocation to a more defensive 55%. About two-thirds of his growth stocks are shares of U.S. companies. One-third of his 18% stake in foreign stocks is spread among emerging markets, including Malaysia, India and Brazil. Says Beckwitt: "The best way to capitalize on emerging economies is to go with a little bit in a lot." He's tucked away half his fixed-income holdings in Treasury bills and the rest in Treasury bonds and high-yield junk bonds. Says Beckwitt: "With no recession in sight, I'm earning four to five percentage points more in junk than in Treasuries."

CGM Mutual. Military buff Ken Heebner isn't about to sound the retreat because of the shellacking his CGM Mutual has suffered over the past 12 months. Down 3%, this balanced fund recently ranked in the bottom percentile of balanced funds. Even worse, $400 million CGM Capital Development Fund, which Heebner also manages, fell 17% into the bottom percentile of growth funds. The impetus? Wrongly figuring that interest rates would not rise, Heebner moved roughly half of CGM Mutual's 75% stock stake into banks and housing-related stocks and the other 25% into long-term bonds. The portfolio got hammered as the Federal Reserve jacked up rates to forestall inflation. "I was not prepared for sharp rate hikes," admits the battered fund general. "It was a mistake." But Heebner has recovered from seemingly crippling losses before. Both CGM Mutual and Capital Development, which is closed to new investors, ranked in the bottom 2% of their categories in 1988, before rebounding to the top 11% and 5%, respectively, over the next three years. Moreover, CGM Mutual has gained 13% annually over the past five years and 15% over 10 years, placing it in the top 5% of its peers. Capital Development ranks in the top 1% of growth funds for those periods. Heebner has moved roughly 45% of his money into stocks, such as $25 billion computer firm Hewlett-Packard, that he believes can increase profits by at least 20% a year. He's put another 30% or so of his assets in battered banks and REITs (real estate investment trusts), expecting their prices will soar as the U.S. economy continues its strong growth. Wary of getting burned again in long-term bonds, Heebner has invested the final 25% in two-year Treasuries for a secure 6% return. And he's confident that most of the volatility fund shareholders see over the next few years will be up, not down. Says he: "I'm very optimistic about my portfolio." Investors who scrutinize the entire opus of Heebner and our other comeback candidates should have good reason to feel the same way.

▶ *The Prudent Way to Profit Overseas*

The most compelling reasons to invest part of your retirement savings abroad are the prospect of superior returns and, surprisingly, a smoother ride. Since prices of foreign shares don't usually rise and fall in sync with U.S. stocks, you can significantly reduce your portfolio's overall risk by diversifying into overseas funds. Let's say that in 1985 you put 70% of your money in U.S. stocks and split the remainder evenly between shares traded on emerging and fully developed foreign stock markets. Ten years later you would have gained 16% annually, vs. 14% for an All American portfolio. And you would have taken 10% less risk.

Below are some of the best buys in three categories of foreign funds. Diversified overseas funds tend to divide their assets among a broad range of regions and countries. Diversified emerging markets funds spread holdings among less developed nations. And regional emerging markets funds specialize in rapidly growing economies in a particular area, such as Asia or Latin America. When investing your retirement money, stick to the widely diversified funds if you don't have the strong stomach to digest temporary price dips of 20% or more. If you do venture into riskier regional markets funds, limit them to 25% of your overseas holdings.

Diversified overseas funds. By spreading their money among a wide number of markets, these funds sharply reduce your chances of being hammered if one or two fall apart. Even so, you should expect occasional years in which most foreign funds get pounded, as happened in 1994. Start by considering Warburg Pincus International (described earlier on page 91), T. Rowe Price International, which holds stocks from 28 countries, and Templeton Foreign, which divvies up its holdings among 37 nations. Banking on Europe's economic recovery, T. Rowe Price's investment team, led by Martin Wade, has put more than 50% of the fund's assets into European countries such as the United Kingdom, France and the Netherlands. Wade has also sunk about 15% of the fund's money into Pacific Rim emerging markets, including Malaysia and Singapore, where he's finding shares that are cheaply priced relative to their strong earnings potential. Templeton Foreign manager Mark Holowesko is looking to increase the 20% or so he has already invested in emerging markets such as Argentina and Mexico to help take advantage of the rebound that he expects to follow on 1994's disappointing returns.

Another recommendation is Vanguard International Growth, partly because the fund holds annual expenses to a razor-thin 0.5% of assets. Vanguard manager Richard Foulkes keeps two-thirds of his portfolio in growth stocks, mostly in developed nations in Asia and Europe. But he is looking to raise his recent 17% stake in fast-growing countries such as Indonesia, Malaysia and Singapore because he believes they are "doing everything right to move from poverty to economic health."

You can shoot for higher international returns with a fund that specializes in the shares of small and mid-size companies. Try T. Rowe Price International Discovery and Tweedy Browne Global Value. The Discovery management team's emphasis on small companies with median market capitalizations of $500 million, plus its 44% stake in emerging markets, has made the fund almost 20% more volatile than large cappers over the past five years. But the extra risk seems to be worth taking because the fund offers shareholders a way to capitalize on the superior gains of small-cap international stocks. Tweedy Browne's quartet of managers specialize in the issues of medium-size companies with $1.3 billion median market capitalizations that sell at a discount to book value or have below-market PEs (price-earnings ratios). The fund, which shies away from most emerging markets, recently had concentrated most of its assets in developed countries ranging from the Netherlands and Switzerland to Hong Kong and Japan.

Diversified emerging markets funds. Keep in mind that they invest in stocks that can zoom to staggering gains one year and suffer bloodcurdling losses the next. For example, Turkish stocks rose 208% in 1993 but fell 53% the following year. So hop aboard only if you would feel comfortable weathering temporary setbacks that could make the 1987 U.S. market crash seem like a stumble. One recommendation is Templeton Developing Markets run by veteran Mark Mobius. A value investor who waits for bargains, Mobius lately had roughly 32% of his assets temporarily in cash, biding his time until he's ready to move into such untested markets as Nigeria and Russia. He's invested the remaining 68% in a broad range of emerging markets, with the largest portions in Hong Kong (17%), Brazil (7%) and Turkey (5%). "These countries are working on their problems," says Mobius. "We think there are good opportunities there."

Regional emerging markets funds. You can earn the loftiest long-term returns, if you're willing to assume equally high risks, by buying one or two funds that invest solely in a promising region's emerging markets. Most analysts caution against jumping into Latin American funds at this point, however. A major reason is that foreign investors will continue to keep their money out of the region until Mexico clearly gets its economic problems under control. Favor instead Asia's battered markets, which figure to produce returns over time that are high enough to compensate you for the added risk of investing in them. Two recommendations are T. Rowe Price New Asia and Scudder Pacific. New Asia team leader Martin Wade says that in recent months he has concentrated most of the fund's money in the stock markets of Malaysia (22%) and Hong Kong (21%). But he's eyeing Korea (5%) because he believes the country's profit potential in exports is especially bright now that the strong yen has jacked up the price of Japanese products. Scudder Pacific, managed by Elizabeth Allan, also holds large stakes in Hong Kong (17%) and Malaysia (13%). But she is branching out into smaller fast-growing Asian markets, such as India (8%) and Indonesia (6%).

▶ *Great Funds to Generate Income*

With the U.S. economy slowing and inflation apparently restrained, short-term interest rates should inch up no more than half a percentage point from 5.75% recently. And long-term rates could drift down below 6%. As a result, you will have no trouble finding bond or high-dividend stock funds with solid yields that won't subject your principal to stomach-churning losses. Investors should be able to make 7% or more in bond funds over the next year. That's nearly a 4% payout after inflation, vs. the 3% cushion of recent years. If you diversify into such income-oriented fund groups as equity income, utility and real estate, you can aim for total returns approaching 10%. Thus you can readily put together a portfolio that will throw off income as well as the growth you need for inflation protection.

Money-market funds. They're the perfect place to stash your emergency cash or money you plan to move into stock or bond funds when you spot an enticing opportunity. Money fund yields, which were lately averaging around 5.5%, are at levels not seen in years. Top performers include Strong Money Market and Jackson National Money Market, both of which have bumped up their yields an extra half-point or so by temporarily waiving management fees.

Short-term taxable bond funds. They can boost your yield a full percentage point or more above money fund payouts. Good choices are Strong Short-Term Bond and Vanguard Fixed-Income Short-Term Corporate. Such funds typically limit themselves to bonds that mature in one to four years. The portfolios' short-term maturities reduce your chances of losing principal if interest rates rise. Beware of funds that try to juice up yields with toxic derivative securities, a strategy that threw some short-term funds for double-digit losses in 1994. You should check the prospectus to make sure the fund's manager is using derivatives solely to hedge interest-rate risk, not to pick up extra yield.

Intermediate taxable bond funds. Consider only those funds that are holding bonds maturing in five to 10 years. That way, you can pick up more than 80% of the yield of long-term bonds while taking on only about 40%

of the interest-rate risk. Indeed, intermediate funds recently yielded about 6%, on average, just over a percentage point less than the payout on 30-year Treasury bonds. What's more, a one-point jump in rates would shave just 5% off a five-year bond's value, vs. 8% off the price of its 30-year counterpart. Investors looking to ride intermediates' relatively secure yields should consider Vanguard Fixed-Income Intermediate-Term Corporate, Fidelity Intermediate Bond and Warburg Pincus Fixed-Income.

Tax-exempt bond funds. If you are in the 28% federal income tax bracket or higher, be sure to check out funds specializing in municipal bonds. (For advice on buying individual bonds, see "Get a Better Deal on Tax-Free Munis" later in this chapter.) They offer tempting tax-free yields that lately averaged 5%. That's the taxable equivalent of 7.3% for someone in the 31% bracket. You can lower your risk exposure by considering only funds that invest in issues maturing in fewer than five years, such as Vanguard Municipal Short-Term Bond Fund and T. Rowe Price Tax-Free Short-Intermediate. If you can stand a bit more volatility, however, you can pick up nearly half a percentage point in yield with intermediate-term munis, such as Dreyfus Intermediate Muni, USAA Tax-Exempt Intermediate-Term and Vanguard Muni Intermediate-Term.

Convertible bond funds. These funds hold preferred stocks or bonds that can be converted into the issuer's common shares. The funds offer steady income plus capital gains if the underlying stock rises in price. Setbacks in both stocks and bonds in 1994 pounded convertibles for a 4% loss. But rising stock prices and stable interest rates could propel these funds to annual returns averaging 10%. Conservatively managed funds to consider are Fidelity Convertible Securities and Franklin Convertible Securities.

High-yield corporate funds. These higher-risk funds invest in securities rated below investment grade by services like Standard & Poor's and Moody's. But if you stick to funds that buy bonds rated just below investment quality, you can grab yields of 8% to 9% without putting your portfolio in jeopardy. Favor such portfolios as Fidelity Capital & Income and Vanguard Fixed-Income High Yield Corporate that largely limit themselves to the top of the junk pile and lower risk further by putting no more than 5% of their assets in a single issue. Still, if the economy slips into recession, even these funds could take a big hit. So conservative investors should keep only a small portion of their bond portfolio in high-yield funds.

Equity income funds. These portfolios generally hold both dividend-paying stocks and bonds. That combination reduces payouts. But their stockholdings give you an opportunity for inflation-beating capital growth. For the past five years, equity income funds' annualized returns beat the rate of inflation by more than six percentage points. For income and capital growth, check out Fidelity Puritan, Lindner Dividend, T. Rowe Price Equity-Income and Vanguard Equity-Income.

Real estate mutual funds. Another inflation hedge, real estate funds typically buy shares of REITs (real estate investment trusts), property developers and home-building companies. Even though REITs have underperformed the market lately, their prospects are improving because of a lack of new construction combined with increasing demand for commercial properties. Two funds that have the potential for producing solid double-digit returns are Cohen & Steers Realty Shares and CGM Realty.

Utility funds. Investing in utilities is complicated by regulatory changes that are ending electric power companies' longtime monopolies in many local markets. Thus investors should focus on funds that spread their holdings over several types of utilities (for example, electric, gas, water and telephone service). Such funds have the potential to return roughly 10% annually. To plug into these gains, investors can consider Vanguard

Specialized Utilities Income Fund, which divvies up its holdings among telecommunications firms and electric, gas and water utilities. Also look at Fortress Utility Fund, which keeps two-thirds of its assets in utilities and the rest in convertible bonds and cash, and the slightly more volatile American Gas Index Fund, which owns shares in natural gas companies across the U.S.

▶ *Get a Better Deal on Tax-Free Munis*

The market for tax-free municipal bonds, traditionally among the most popular investments for retirees, can be enigmatic. You can't find prices for most tax-exempt bonds in the newspaper. If you call several brokers, you are likely to get different quotes for the same muni. You never know exactly how much your dealer is earning on the trade because his commission is built into the price. And if the city, county or agency that issued your bond ever runs into financial trouble, chances are you'll probably hear about it first on the evening news—just as investors did in troubled Orange County, California.

Under pressure from regulators, the municipal bond industry is taking steps to help individuals find out more about yields, prices and the fiscal health of issuers. The changes come just in time to help muni investors profit. Muni bonds got clobbered by rising interest rates in 1994. Prices fell an average of 10% among munis that receive the highest AAA rating for quality by bond services such as Moody's and Standard & Poor's. But those bonds regained much of that lost ground in 1995 and should continue to remain attractive for many investors.

The outlook isn't totally sunny. Munis could get hit with a temporary setback if Orange County, which filed for bankruptcy after losing some $1.7 billion in risky investments, has to delay paying off any of the $1.3 billion in notes that are coming due. Nevertheless, tax-free bonds are a good choice for investors in the 31% federal tax bracket or higher. Fewer than 1% of munis have ever defaulted, whereas the default rate for corporate bonds ranges from 1.4% per decade for AAA bonds to 5.7% per decade for those rated triple B, the lowest grade that is still considered investment quality. And they can produce decidedly juicier payouts because munis are free from federal tax (and also from state and local taxes if they are issued in your state). A 10-year AAA insured muni, for instance, was recently paying roughly 5%, the equivalent of a taxable yield of 7.3% for someone in the 31% federal tax bracket. That was about one full percentage point higher than the yield on comparable Treasuries. For people in the 36% and 39.6% brackets, the tax-equivalent yields were even higher (7.9% and 8.4%, respectively).

Those advantages are particularly important to people with enough money to create a diversified portfolio of individual bonds. Such people could always invest in a muni fund, of course. But a fund's yield and credit quality shift as the manager buys and sells bonds. Moreover, because funds don't have a fixed maturity, you can lose some money if you bail out after interest rates have risen (all bonds lose value when rates rise and gain value when rates fall). The buyer of individual issues, on the other hand, can ride out market swings by simply holding the bonds until they mature—provided you bought highly reliable issues on reasonable terms in the first place.

The problem with buying individual bonds today is that you practically have to be a professional to find the best deals. There are some 50,000 issuers and 1.5 million different securities in circulation. Yet the muni market is thinner than those numbers suggest. Only 180 or so issues trade actively on any given day. If you're looking for a specific bond and your broker doesn't happen to have it, he would either offer you a substitute or buy the bond from another dealer. And there's no central exchange where buyers and sellers meet, so he may not be able to find it. As a result, investors have tended to buy whatever their brokerage firm happened to have in its inventory, at whatever price that was quoted, without knowing whether they were getting a good deal.

How reforms help investors. The current efforts won't remedy the problem of limited inventory, but they will make it harder for brokers to overcharge you. Under a new price-quote program offered by J.J. Kenny, you can get prices for specific bonds by calling 800-BOND-INF and giving the bond's multidigit Cusip number (get it from your broker, your monthly statement or the bond itself) or else its coupon rate, maturity, issuer and date of issue. You'll get the bond's price, which includes the broker's commission, based on recent trades of that bond or similar issues. The $10 fee is charged to your credit card. And if you don't need all 25 price quotes that day, call back as often as you like to collect the rest.

The Kenny system isn't flawless. Valuations are based on trades totaling $1 million in value, the standard lot for large transactions (and the price used to derive the valuations on your brokerage statement). But personal trades usually involve smaller quantities, so you can expect to pay about 2% to 3% more than the Kenny price if you're buying a bond and to receive that much less if you're selling. Still, the price-quote system will let you know if the broker's price is in the right ball park and, if it's not, may help you talk him down. You may even be able to reduce the premium below 2% if you are a regular customer or if the broker is eager for your future business.

Your broker too has better price data these days, which will work to your benefit in the long run. The Municipal Securities Rulemaking Board, the industry's self-regulatory group, has been collecting information on dealer-to-dealer trades and distributing it to investment professionals through data services like Kenny and Bloomberg. Over the next few years, the MSRB will expand its tracking to include retail trades. None of this information was available before. It should help smooth out the price disparities that now exist in the dealer-to-dealer market and thus help make more uniform the prices small investors pay. Your dealer will think twice before quoting you an inflated price because he knows his competitors may be selling the same bond for less.

▶ *Wield Your PC for Bigger Returns*

Anyone who knows Jack Alwen of suburban Portland, Ore. would hoot if you described him as a computer nerd. At 68, the retired auto executive and avid golfer spends more time on the links than on-line—and prefers it that way. Yet Alwen is among the growing army of investors who use personal computers to invest smarter, more efficiently and more profitably. Working just a few minutes each evening on his $2,000 Gateway computer, he downloads share prices for the 15 funds he owns. Then he graphs their performance against the market and judges what to buy or sell. Alwen credits this routine with helping him manage a gain of 63% since he started investing by computer in 1990, well ahead of the S&P 500 index's corresponding 46% rise. Indeed, the ritual is so ingrained that when he and his wife Mary took a few days' vacation recently, he jokes, "I was lost without my machine."

You may not need to track your retirement portfolio daily, as Alwen does. But if you think about your funds only once a year, a computer can help you make some decisions by providing a bounty of data on performance, risks and expenses that was once available only to investment professionals. It's still up to you, of course, to supply the prudent judgment. But we show how selected software and on-line services can help make those judgments easier. To use these products, all you need is a reasonably modern computer ($1,200 and up in today's market), a modem ($80 to $200) and the urge to be a more successful investor.

Compute your portfolio's results. Keeping current on your portfolio's value is a simple chore for your computer but a valuable one for you, especially if you own funds from several families and reinvest dividends and gains. To track your portfolio, the computer fetches up-to-date price quotes via modem for each of your funds and totals up your holdings. The noncomputer alternative is to go through newspaper listings and multiply each fund's closing price by the number of shares you own. Without these periodic updates, you don't know your portfolio's exact value (which may be eye-opening in itself). You can't be sure whether you have a gain or a loss on any individual fund (which affects your tax strategy). Most important, you can't tell whether your portfolio still conforms to the asset allocation you intended.

The quick way to get tracking is to open an account with one of the commercial on-line services, such as America Online, Compuserve or Prodigy (see "Comparing Computer Investing Tools" on page 107 for prices and descriptions of the products mentioned here). All three offer portfolio update services as part of their basic monthly charge. Of the three, we prefer the simplicity of America Online. From its Quotes & Portfolios menu, you can find the latest price for any of more than 5,000 funds simply by entering the investment's name or ticker symbol. Once the quote appears on your screen, you can click a button titled "add to portfolio" to append it to a ledger of as many as 100 issues. Thereafter, whenever you open your portfolio the computer automatically will show the latest price available for each item plus the aggregate value of your holdings and your net loss or gain.

If you're serious about following your fund portfolio by computer, however, the on-line services won't satisfy you for long. They make no provision for reinvested dividends. You have to create a separate portfolio entry for each purchase. A dedicated fund investor probably will be happier with personal finance software such as *Quicken* ($40 to $60), *Managing Your Money* ($40 to $60) and *Wealth Builder* ($60). All three allow you to hook up with on-line information sources to download daily quotes, and all let you organize the data more or less as you want it. For example, *Quicken,* the biggest seller of the three, lets you create separate portfolios for your various accounts—IRA, 401(k)s and so forth. It handles reinvested dividends and gains with ease. It produces written reports or graphs of your investment performance. And when you sell, it supplies the data you need to complete Schedule D, the tax form for reporting capital losses or gains. You can also transfer the data from *Quicken* (or from any of its rivals) to most popular tax preparation programs.

There is one main drawback to tracking your portfolio on *Quicken* or its brethren. If you want the program to calculate the tax cost of funds you already own, you'll have to enter your transaction history manually, which could take hours. If you would rather not bother, try calling the fund companies where you have accounts and asking them to compute the average cost of your shares. Then enter the number of shares you own and their average cost as your opening balance for each new fund account. Henceforth, you can record reinvested dividends and capital gains normally. The program keeps an accurate tally of your tax basis provided you use the average cost method of calculating your basis as well as your gain or loss.

Shop for funds electronically. Suppose you are looking for a good small-cap growth fund with stable management, low expenses and above-average gains at below-average risk. You have two choices. You can camp out in the library and comb through financial publications looking for that special fund. Or you could let your computer search quickly through nearly all of today's fund names and find the handful that qualify. Computer screening programs, which allow you to sift through a large database of funds to locate those that fit your precise needs, have elevated fund picking from a shot in the dark to an almost scientific endeavor. Once only mainframes had the power to handle screens. Now a dozen screening programs costing anywhere from $25 to $290 run contentedly on late-model home PCs.

If you think 12b-1 is a vitamin, stick with programs for novices, such as Intuit's *Your Mutual Fund Selector*. This program, available as a $30 CD-ROM or bundled free with *Quicken Deluxe* ($60), begins by interviewing you to determine your assets, goals and risk tolerance. It then produces a pie chart showing how you should

Comparing Computer Investing Tools

Investing software will cost you between $30 and $60 initially plus $45 to $225 a year for periodic data updates. Products and on-line services are listed below in the sequence in which they appear in this chapter.

PRODUCT	PRICE[1]	AVAILABLE FOR	NO. OF FUNDS	COMMENTS
America Online	$10 a month	Windows, DOS, Mac	5,000+	Investing resources are limited but moderately priced as a rule.
Compuserve	$10 a month	Windows, DOS, Mac	7,000+	You can get the price history of any stock or fund in its large database.
Prodigy	$10 a month	Windows, DOS, Mac	4,000+	Service permits investors to store two separate portfolios on-line.
Quicken/Quicken Deluxe	$40/$60	Windows, DOS, Mac	7,000+[6]	It can automatically debit your checking account for checks written to buy stock.
Wealth Builder	$60[2]	Windows, Mac	4,600+	For $7 a month, it alerts you if your fund makes news you should know about.
Managing Your Money	$40 (CD-ROM: $60)	Windows, DOS, Mac	7,000+[7]	It offers "what if" scenarios to decide which securities to sell to reduce taxes.
Your Mutual Fund Selector	$30[3]	Windows (CD-ROM)	1,000+	The fund list changes quarterly, so buy the service's updates.
Principia/On Floppy	$45 a year[4]	Windows, DOS	6,000+	Program shows the relative weightings by sector for each fund's holdings.
Mutual Fund Expert–Personal	$50 a year[5]	Windows, DOS	6,600+	Service includes some 1,000 money–market funds not in Morningstar.

Notes: [1]Street price (software products) [2]On-line price and fund database updates: $10 a month; $18 a month for stock and bond databases too [3]Plus $40 a year for quarterly data updates [4]Quarterly updates: $95 a year; monthly updates: $195 [5]Quarterly updates: $107 a year; monthly updates: $221 [6]Fund updates available only on-line, except with Deluxe CD-ROM edition [7]Fund updates available only on-line divide your money among various types of funds, and even recommends specific buys from its 1,000-fund database. There's also a primer on funds, where you can find out that 12b-1 is an annual marketing fee.

With *Selector,* even someone who knows nothing about investing can put together a respectable portfolio. For example, if you plugged in information on a hypothetical 30-year-old couple who wanted to save for their child's college education, the program suggests they put 30% of their money in growth-stock funds, 14% in overseas stock funds, 33% in bond funds and the rest in U.S. Treasury bills—a reasonable mix for cautious investors. Experienced investors may find parts of *Selector* a bit silly, however. One video clip features a croupier who deals you a hand of blackjack in a test that's designed to measure your appetite for risk. A more serious drawback is that the program can screen funds based on only 10 criteria, some of which are of dubious value.

If you would rather work with a wider universe of possibilities, check out the packages from Morningstar and Steele Systems. These are for serious fund pickers. Morningstar's *Principia* and *On Floppy* and Steele's *Mutual Fund Expert–Personal* all let you roam a database of more than 6,000 funds. Cost is around $100 a year if you get quarterly data updates. Another screening program is *Wealth Builder* by Reality Online. It includes a portfolio tracking feature and a database of 4,600 funds supplied by Morningstar that you can update on-line daily for $10 a month. It also aspires to be a complete financial planning package, covering stocks, bonds, money markets and CDs.

The principal drawback to such screening programs (except *Selector*) is that you need to know what to screen for. If you don't, but would like to learn, try joining an investment club that focuses on computers. The American Association of Individual Investors sponsors a bunch. Membership is $49 a year (call 800-428-2244). It also publishes a bimonthly newsletter, *Computerized Investing,* ($30 annually for members, $40 nonmembers) that reviews investing software and on-line services.

5

Make the Most of Your Real Estate

*F*or most middle-income people, the process of trading up or improving on their homes is the foundation of family wealth and retirement planning. They began their housing quest deep in debt and, thanks to inflation, ended up with a tidy treasure that often can be tapped absolutely tax-free to buttress retirement income from other sources. How so? If you or your spouse are 55 or older, you may be eligible to exclude from taxes up to $125,000 of capital gains on the sale of your primary residence. Should your gain exceed $125,000, you can defer tax on the excess by reinvesting the money in a new home. If you have lived in your house for fewer than three of the five years preceding the sale, you do not qualify for the exclusion. In that case, it's probably worth delaying the sale until you can take the tax break.

About 75% of Americans over 65 own their own homes, with an average of more than $50,000 in equity (the market price minus one's outstanding mortgage) waiting to be tapped. Most retirees living on fixed incomes, however, don't earn enough to qualify for conventional home equity loans, the simplest way to exploit this burgeoning asset. But selling out and buying (or renting) a smaller place, known as trading down, is usually the smartest move anyway. On balance, it also outperforms such alternatives as just staying put or taking a reverse mortgage, which is a loan against home equity that allows the borrower to defer repayment (see "Living off Your Old Homestead" on page 112). What's best for you depends on whether you need to raise money from your home and how much. If your income from investments, Social Security, pensions and other sources falls well short of your requirements, you may have precious little choice but to tap your prime asset.

▶ Get the Best Price for Your Home

It wasn't so long ago that rock-bottom mortgage rates of roughly 6.8%, coupled with a strong economy, sent hordes of home shoppers knocking on the doors of empty nesters and retirees who were more than delighted to see them. Now, however, a slower economy and higher 8% mortgage rates have thinned the crowds considerably. The National Association of Realtors expects annual home sales to slump to 4.3 million units, down nearly 6% from 1994's post-recession high of 4.6 million units. With demand lessening, prices are likely to remain flat, disappointing sellers. According to the NAR, prices generally will keep pace with inflation, rising about 3.5% annually thanks to big projected gains in such hot markets as Portland, Ore. and Salt Lake City. Meanwhile, whatever benefit buyers get from soft prices is likely to be absorbed by today's higher mortgage costs.

For a forecast of what's in store for housing where you live, see our housing market ranking on page 114. No. 1 Portland, where house prices rose an estimated 10.8% in 1994, towers above the crowd with a 9.7% hike projected for 1995. Among the reasons cited are expansion of the area's computer-based manufacturing industries and a steady stream of house-hungry refugees pouring in from such megacities as Los Angeles. Just behind Portland rank the Salt Lake City/Ogden metro area (7.8%), followed by Orlando (5.4%), San Antonio (4.7%), Fort Lauderdale (4.5%) and Greensboro/Winston-Salem, N.C. (4.4%).

With Portland's economic strengths, it's hardly surprising that the metro area's home prices lately were $14,000 above the U.S. median of $102,575. Happily for buyers elsewhere, median prices in half of the 10 hottest housing markets fall below the U.S. figure. The five most afford-

Living off Your Old Homestead

If you've owned your home for 20 years or more, you occupy a rich storehouse of cash that can be tapped for retirement expenses. To get your hands on it, you could trade down, selling your house and buying (or renting) one that costs less. If you'd prefer to stay in your house, however, there's an alternative known as a reverse mortgage. With such a loan, you pledge your home as collateral at your local bank in exchange for cash—a monthly stipend, a lump sum, a line of credit or a combination of the three. You don't pay back the loan's principal and interest until you move out or die.

▶ **How reverse mortgages work.** To qualify for one, you must own your home or condominium free or nearly free of debt. Some lenders require you to be at least 62, but there are no income limits. Here's the basic deal. Let's say a 72-year-old woman owns a $120,000 house. Her lender would be willing to advance her a $49,000 lump sum, using a formula based on her life expectancy, her home's value and the lender's cost of making the loan. Or the lender would instead pay her $335 a month for as long as she lived in the house. Or she could take out a line of credit for $49,000 and draw on it as needed.

▶ **Factor in your life expectancy.** The older you are, the more you typically can borrow. That's because your life expectancy (and the loan term) will be shorter. If you and your spouse own your home jointly, some lenders will use your joint life expectancy in calculating the loan amount. Others will base it on the younger spouse's age. You'll be charged annual interest, lately around 8% compounded monthly, which you or your estate will pay when the loan comes due. That same year, you or your estate can take a tax deduction for the total interest. In addition, the lender will charge you closing costs of $2,000 to $4,000.

▶ **Add on the cost of insurance.** Reverse mortgages guarantee that the loan will never cost more than the value of your home even if that value drops before payment is due. Lenders usually take out insurance against such losses and stick borrowers with the premium. You should probably figure on about 2% of the home's value, payable when the loan commences, plus 0.5% a year. If you're forced to move, say, to a nursing home, the loan comes due immediately. In addition, the lender will demand its money if you default for reasons that apply to any mortgage, such as failure to pay your property taxes or keep your home in salable condition. Your lender could default too, of course, on monthly payments to you. So you should stick to federally insured institutions.

able all have strong local economies (Salt Lake City, Orlando, San Antonio, Greensboro/Winston-Salem, N.C., and Phoenix). And their respective regions are attracting plenty of new residents. To help you come out ahead whether you're on the selling or buying end of the deal, here are answers to the questions that cover key issues you need to consider in today's tepid housing market.

How do I set an asking price? The price should be your best estimate of the house's true market value. In the current environment, it's not smart for sellers to play games. An inflated price could cause your home to languish. After a month or more, it may seem like damaged goods, and you may be compelled to accept less than you could have gotten earlier. Even in a fairly robust market, overreaching may scare off buyers who simply can't swing the extra mortgage payments. To get the price right, don't depend on one appraisal from a real estate agent, who might boost the figure to get your business or, worse, lower it to earn a quick commission. Instead, get estimates from several agents. Then check the price yourself by looking up recent home sales in your local newspaper or county register. Note the selling prices of houses similar to yours in location, size and amenities (called comparables in the trade) and set your price accordingly.

Should I try to sell my own house? If you don't have much equity in your home, you may be tempted to sell it yourself to save the 6% commission most brokers extract. But try to bear in mind that only about 20% of all homes are sold by their owners, a figure that has remained fairly constant for 10 years. Let's face it, few owners are prepared to sort the browsers from the serious prospects and close the deal. Without a broker, you also will be shut out of the multiple listing system run by your local Board of Realtors. If, however, you are comfortable playing salesman, peddling your own home can work out fine. Desirable, well-priced homes often sell themselves anyway. What's more, if you don't have to factor in a commission, you can even price your home a

What's Hot and Not in Housing Markets

House prices are expected to spurt 9.7% this year in Portland, Ore. but rise less than 4% in most other big metro areas.

RANK	METROPOLITAN AREA	PROJECTED ANNUAL GAIN	MEDIAN PRICE	ANNUAL INCOME NEEDED[1]
1	Portland, Ore.	9.7%	$116,190	$30,593
2	Salt Lake City	7.8	94,950	25,665
3	Orlando	5.4	91,300	22,503
4	San Antonio	4.7	78,470	20,380
5	Fort Lauderdale	4.5	102,890	25,168
6	Greensboro/Winston-Salem, N.C.	4.4	92,910	23,968
7	Phoenix	4.4	90,400	23,898
8	Denver	4.3	112,980	29,479
9	Charlotte, N.C.	4.3	104,120	27,147
10	Middlesex/Somerset counties, N.J.	4.2	176,930	44,629
11	Tampa/St. Petersburg	4.1	74,940	18,261
12	Nashville	4.0	94,370	25,301
13	Atlanta	3.8	91,900	23,441
14	Memphis	3.8	86,520	23,268
15	Houston	3.8	80,220	21,400
16	Chicago	3.8	141,750	37,205
17	Seattle	3.8	153,170	40,166
18	St. Louis	3.8	85,970	22,330
19	Columbus, Ohio	3.7	95,850	25,307
20	Minneapolis	3.6	99,360	26,690
21	Fort Worth	3.6	82,220	22,057
22	Dallas	3.5	94,960	25,203
23	Boston	3.4	178,720	44,493
24	Washington, D.C.	3.3	155,600	40,048
25	Milwaukee	3.3	108,260	28,758

RANK	METROPOLITAN AREA	PROJECTED ANNUAL GAIN	MEDIAN PRICE	ANNUAL INCOME NEEDED[1]
26	Kansas City, Mo.	3.2	85,300	22,112
27	Newark	3.2	188,180	46,897
28	Cleveland/Lorain/Elyria	3.2	97,090	25,432
29	Sacramento	3.2	124,800	32,594
	U.S. median	3.2	102,575	26,676
30	Detroit	3.1	84,360	22,805
31	Indianapolis	3.0	90,730	23,712
32	Monmouth/Ocean counties, N.J.	3.0	134,090	33,860
33	Miami	3.0	102,210	25,575
34	Baltimore	2.8	118,060	30,749
35	Orange County, Calif.	2.7	212,270	56,477
36	Riverside/San Bernardino, Calif.	2.7	129,510	34,776
37	New Orleans	2.7	76,520	20,289
38	Cincinnati	2.6	94,170	24,641
39	Bergen/Passaic counties, N.J.	2.6	190,390	47,339
40	New York City	2.5	172,390	42,759
41	Rochester, N.Y.	2.5	86,490	22,254
42	San Francisco	2.4	250,270	65,078
43	New Haven/Bridgeport, Conn.	2.3	142,020	34,230
44	Nassau/Suffolk counties, N.Y.	2.3	157,670	39,525
45	Buffalo/Niagara Falls	2.1	81,160	20,466
46	Norfolk/Virginia Beach	2.1	102,260	26,662
47	Philadelphia	1.7	116,640	29,400
48	Hartford	1.5	132,330	30,844
49	San Diego	1.5	177,340	46,603
50	Los Angeles/Long Beach	1.0	184,900	44,891

Notes and sources: [1]Annual income needed to buy a house in each of the 50 largest metro areas assumes a 20% down payment, a 30-year loan term, and that no more than 30% of a household's income is used for the monthly mortgage payment. This analysis was prepared for MONEY by Regional Financial Associates, West Chester, Pa.

bit below the competition and still come out ahead. For $200 or so, you may be able to list your place in a directory of homes being sold by their owners. About 200 entrepreneurs around the country publish such guides. If you're undecided about whether to sell solo, check the video *How to Sell Your Own Home* ($29; 800-836-5577).

How can I spruce up my home? You should concentrate on first-impression improvements, such as washing all your windows, uncluttering closets, installing higher-wattage light bulbs to brighten the rooms and upgrading the hardware on your front door. For a few dollars more, homeowners might consider painting dirty walls and planting flowers. You must, however, make obviously needed repairs. A dripping faucet, broken railing, rusty mailbox or malfunctioning lock signal wary buyers that your home isn't well-maintained. If anyone makes a bid at all, it will be at a "handyman's special" price. More worrisome signs, such as odors from a leaky oil furnace or a telltale whine in the central air conditioner, are sure to scare off prospective buyers altogether.

What should I bid if I'm buying? Comparables will help here too. In a buyer's market (defined as one where prices are dropping or barely moving), you can play hardball and bid 5% or so below the comparable, particularly if the house has been on the market for a few months. In a seller's market, where prices could be increasing 7% or more annually, dickering probably won't help. Try instead to make a bid 2% below the asking price if you can pay cash, already have a mortgage commitment or can promise a quick close.

Should I get a fixed or adjustable loan? Grab a fixed rate. Mortgages with adjustable rates can rise as much as two points a year and six points over the life of the loan. But the rate on a 30-year fixed mortgage, lately around 8%, is only two percentage points higher than that on the typical ARM. Unless you like to gamble, that's a small price to pay for stability. An adjustable rate can make sense if you plan to move within two or three years or if you can't afford a fixed rate on your retirement income. There are many adjustable choices, however, so shop around. Fairly new options are five-year and 10-year ARMs, which offer a fixed rate for that initial period then readjust yearly. They cost more than standard ARMs but provide a lot more predictability.

Is a buyer's broker a good idea? That depends on how informed and assertive a buyer you are. Unlike the traditional agent who looks out for the seller, a buyer's broker acts as your advocate, helping you find the home you want and then negotiating the lowest possible price. The best buyer's brokers are so-called exclusive agents who represent only buyers, never sellers, and thus are not tempted to push a house on which they stand to earn a commission. A true buyer's broker will bring to your attention a house's subtle flaws, such as an outdated property assessment that may mean sharply higher tax bills down the line. And you will be coached on how to get price cuts or concessions from the seller. Depending on the help offered, a buyer's broker might charge $60 to $125 an hour or, more typically, 2% to 3% of the price of the house you buy. Although an expert negotiator can usually trim a home's selling price more than you would be able to on your own, there are no guarantees. Furthermore, there are few standards regulating such brokers. One helpful sign is that a broker has completed a certification course, such as the one offered by the Real Estate Buyer Agency Council, a professional group. You can find a true buyer's broker in most states by calling Buyer's Resource (800-359-4092) and stipulating that you want an exclusive agent.

▶ *Roomier Returns on Properties*

Perhaps the most heartening news for aspiring retirees is that the market for residential rentals, which was left for dead after the housing recession of the late 1980s, is coming back to life. If you have $10,000 or more to invest, the revival offers some of the best tax write-offs around. There also are opportunities to earn 10% or more annually in combined income and capital gains. And unlike stocks and bonds, whose returns are out of your control, you can actually boost a rental property's market value through shrewd management and imaginative remodeling.

Today's tight rental market is a major plus. "Demand for rentals is rising steadily, but there's been very little new construction since the 1986 Tax Act curtailed builders' and investors' ability to take some tax write-offs," says Michael Sampson, professor of taxation at American University and author of *Tax Guide for Residential Real Estate*. The residential vacancy rate, a vital indicator of the health of the local rental market, has slimmed down to a lean 3% or less in far-flung cities including Austin, Denver, Nashville, Raleigh and Salt Lake City. Nationwide, the vacancy rate has dropped from a 20-year high of 8% in 1987 to 7.3% lately.

In many areas of the country, the lack of rental units is propelling rents higher. As a result, your chances of buying a building with a positive cash flow (where rental income exceeds expenses) are better than at any time since the late 1980s. You don't have endless time to catch the action, however. Property prices, mortgage rates and rents have been edging higher. Furthermore, builders are literally hammering away to meet the demand. As new units come to market, they will tend to increase competition for desirable tenants and hamper landlords' ability to raise rents. So get to know brokers who have worked in your neighborhood for a long time, ask them what they see ahead for your area, and then start shopping for properties.

Before embracing a rental investment, however, you need to make sure that you or your partner possess a landlord's temperament. "My wife doesn't mind calls about broken pipes. But I'm less than thrilled," concedes Kenneth Edwards of Corvallis, Ore. Edwards, the author of *Homebuyer's Survival Guide*, checks out the finances on potential properties while leaving the plumbing patrol to his wife Judith. Also follow these general guidelines.

Tot up potential tax advantages. No matter
where you live, the tax benefits for rental real estate are
still enticing. Middle-income investors have a terrific
edge over property plutocrats. If your adjusted gross
income (AGI) is less than $100,000, you can write off
against earned income as much as $25,000 a year from
rental losses as long as you actively manage your property. That means, for example, setting rents and choosing your tenants. (This tax break phases out until your
AGI hits $150,000, at which point it disappears.) Rental
real estate also offers the nifty deduction of depreciation, which generates a tax write-off without a corresponding cash outlay. For example, if you own a rental
building that is worth $190,000, you can claim deprecia-
tion of about $6,900 a year for 27.5 years—the standard
period for writing off residential property.

Look homeward, investor. Start investigating
neighborhoods that are within a convenient 30-minute
drive of your home. You'll be more familiar with the
market and more apt to keep a hawk eye on your
investment. Go where people are building or fixing up
their houses—both signs that the neighborhood is
improving. Then look at the middle to low end of the
price range where there's more room for appreciation.
In addition, ask local real estate agents for a list of communities that have the shortest resale time for residential
properties. That signals a seller's market, which will
push property values higher. Such increases, in turn,
build your equity while giving you better borrowing
power if you choose to hold the unit long term. Single-
family rental houses take about three months to sell.
Also get your area's local vacancy rate from a knowl-
edgeable real estate agent. If it's hovering around 5%,
you can probably rent your property with ease. At 7%
to 10%, you may have trouble finding topnotch tenants.
Above 10%, drive on by unless the price is right and
you expect the neighborhood to turn around soon.

Think small starting out. "A multifamily house of,

say, two or three units is good for beginning investors," suggests Carolyn Janik, author of the guide *Money-Making Real Estate*. "You learn to interview tenants, set rents, answer complaints and see whether you really want to be a landlord." At the same time, with several units, your rental income won't drop to zero if one tenant decamps unexpectedly. Be wary of most condominiums, however. Michael Sampson warns that condo associations can be notoriously unpredictable for investors. For instance, one Florida group, dominated by retirees, voted to close its swimming pool as an economy measure. "This wrecked the value of the property for the owners who rented their units to vacationing families," he points out. Though condo prices have long been flat owing to overbuilding, they've begun inching higher as sales have picked up. The median price lately was $110,300, supported by strong demand from both retirees and first-time buyers.

Aim for positive cash flow. When you find a property you like, bargain hard and try to pay no more than 80% of market value. You can determine a property's value by checking recent sales prices of comparable dwellings with an appraiser or real estate agent. Your goal is to own a building that provides a positive cash flow, preferably on a pretax basis. Its income ought to pay the bills from the day the place is in rentable condition. To help determine whether a rental property is worth buying, follow the example of American University's Sampson. He asks the current owner for three years' worth of Schedule E tax forms, used to report supplemental income from rental real estate to the IRS. "The landlord will minimize profits and maximize expenses on the Schedule E to reduce taxable profits, so I'm seeing the worst-case scenario," Sampson explains. Also hire a building inspector (cost: $250 to $500) to provide a written report on the property. Then estimate the cost of any needed repairs. Favor situations in which your figures show the improvements will probably pay for themselves over a period of three years or fewer.

To unearth a real bargain, you may have to find a foreclosure, an auction or a seller in distress. Take the case of Brenda Bradsher, who in 1982 bought a three-bedroom house in Houston's Heights section for $20,000 in cash when the owners couldn't come up with $3,000 in back taxes and foreclosure was threatened. "A nearby vacant lot had recently sold for about $45,000, so I knew I couldn't lose," says Bradsher, who runs an industrial hardware supply brokerage. She got a $60,000 home improvement loan to restore the house. After the facelift, it qualified for an $82,000 mortgage, which Bradsher used to repay the first loan—and herself. She now has only $10,000 of her own money invested in the property. That $10,000 lately has earned an unusually roomy return because Bradsher has so little cash tied up in the property. Still, she keeps a sharp eye on the expenses of the three rental buildings that she owns. "After a house is in rentable condition, I want a mini-mum $200-a-month positive cash flow," Bradsher says. "That's enough to rest easy in the event a tenant inflicts unexpected damage."

Crunch these numbers hard. The worksheet on page 122 will guide you through the necessary financial analysis. But you will still need to estimate some variable costs, such as repairs and maintenance. With the worksheet complete, carefully mull two numbers. On line 11, the cash-on-cash return measures the gain on your cash investment. The pros say the return should be at least double the prevailing interest rate on one-year CDs, or around 10%. And on line 14, the return on investment should be at least 10%. To be sure you know what you're getting into, work up a final percent-age called the capitalization rate (it's not in the work-sheet). This figure measures the property's ability to generate a return on your investment. Calculate it by dividing the property's net operating income (line 4 on the worksheet) by its purchase price. The higher the cap rate, the sounder the deal. If the cap rate is less than 8%, you're looking at a relatively risky proposition.

Crunch a Rental's Numbers Like a Pro

If you've zeroed in on a one-family house, a duplex or other prospective rental property investment, try to fill out this worksheet to determine whether to make a bid or walk on by. Two figures pretty much tell all. On line 11, you'll get the annual return you can expect on the cash you invest, once the property is in rentable condition. You want to see at least double the prevailing interest rate on one-year CDs, or roughly 10% or better. On line 14, you'll get the overall projected return on your investment. If that figure works out to be 10% or more, you probably should consider taking the plunge into rental real estate.

1 a) Annual rents $_____
   b) Allowance for vacancies and uncollected rents
       (typically 5%) $_____
2 Net rents (line 1a minus line 1b) $_____
3 Annual deductible operating expenses, excluding mortgage, such as repairs and maintenance (typically 10% of net rents), property taxes, insurance, management fees of 7% to 10% $_____
4 Net operating income before mortgage expense (line 2 minus line 3) $_____
5 Annual mortgage interest payment $_____
6 Annual pretax cash flow (line 4 minus line 5) $_____
7 Annual property depreciation (cost of the building but not the land, divided by 27.5 years) $_____
8 Tax loss or gain (line 6 minus line 7) $_____
9 Annual tax loss or tax due (line 8 multiplied by your combined federal, state and city tax rates) $_____
10 After-tax cash flow (line 6 plus or minus line 9) $_____
11 Cash-on-cash return (line 10 divided by cash invested) _____%
12 Projected one-year gain in price (purchase price multiplied by the estimated 12-month percentage increase in value) $_____
13 Projected total return for year (line 10 plus line 12) $_____
14 Return on investment (line 13 divided by cash invested) _____%

Source: Michael Sampson

▶ *Terrific Places for Energetic Retirees*

The best places to retire are Prescott, Ariz.; Fairhope, Ala.; Mount Dora, Fla.; Las Vegas; and Chapel Hill, N.C. That's the consensus of a board of experts who helped MONEY choose the top retirement locations in the U.S. We asked the experts what retirees want when they relocate. Then we drew up a wish list of attributes, led by low crime rate, mild climate, affordable housing, attractive environment, proximity to cultural and educational activities, strong economic outlook and excellent health care. We then asked the experts to rank the towns in America that best fulfilled the wishes.

You'll find our 12 top choices ranked in the table on page 126, along with the names of our experts. The table cites vital information about each location including cost of living, average home price, tax rates and weather. What these places have in common is an abundance of available activities. That's because our experts find today's retirees to be as energetic as when they had full-time jobs. Indeed, as more people leave the work force younger and stay healthy longer, their idea of retirement is changing. "Retirement used to be viewed as an extended vacation," says Mark Fagan, a professor in social work at Alabama's Jacksonville State University who has studied retirees for a decade. "These days it's seen as an opportunity to pursue neglected hobbies, take a part-time job or become involved in community activities."

Each year about half a million Americans in their sixties make the move to new hometowns. For many this is the first time they have been able to choose a community they actually like, rather than one that is merely close to work, the right schools or a convenient commuter train. And the choice can be most invigorating. "By making a complete change of venue, we could start fresh," says Hugh Chapin, 68, who left Lexington, Mass. with his wife Joan, 62, for a village outside Chapel Hill, N.C. "Retirement wouldn't have been this exciting if we had stayed in the community we had lived in for 40 years."

Before you put down cash for a new house, however, spend six months to a year visiting your prospective new community in as many seasons as possible. You can meet potential neighbors, shop in local markets, sample recreational facilities, get a sense of local politics and feel the fluctuations in the weather. Clear, mild days in Las Vegas, for instance, might seem lovely in February when there are 10 inches of ice and snow back home. But a summer of temperatures consistently over 100° might make you long again for your northern environs. To help you learn what to look for, here are reports on the five retirement places at the top of our list.

Prescott, Arizona. The mild climate and laid-back lifestyle attract more than 600 retirees a year to this mile-high mountain town (population 28,211). Bordered by 1.25 million acres of national forest and the 1,400-acre Yavapai Indian Reservation, Prescott is an ideal spot if you love outdoor activities. Its high elevation and mountain breezes keep temperatures from reaching the grueling levels of low-lying Phoenix, 90 miles to the south. In summer they rarely exceed 85°, and in winter's sun-filled days they average about 50°. Humidity stays a moderate 45% year round. Practically every day, you can play tennis, golf on two city courses, one created by famed designer Gary Panks, or hike along the many trails on nearby Granite Mountain. The Grand Canyon is a two-hour drive away.

Because Prescott is the county seat, many services are conveniently located in town. They include the regional Social Security office, motor vehicles department and 129-bed Yavapai Regional Medical Center. No wonder retirees favor this quiet mountain community. About 23% of the population is over 65, half of them relocated from California and the Rocky Mountain states. The living in Prescott, though bountiful, is not cheap. We estimate that a retired couple need annual income of at least $25,000 to live comfortably.

Founded in 1864 as the territorial capital of Arizona, Prescott still has the distinct feel of a wild West town. Historic Whiskey Row once had 20 raucous saloons.

Today, many of the original buildings house boutiques, hotels and gift shops. The town also had its genteel side, which can be seen in Mount Vernon Street's graceful Victorian homes, many of them on the National Register of Historic Places. "This is a town that attracts individuals," says Peter Dickinson, 67, one of our panelists and a resident since 1988. "There is nothing cookie cutter about it—not the people, not even the homes." Indeed, most of the houses are custom built into the rough and hilly terrain, where wild boars sometimes wander across the yards at night. In many residential developments, builders are required to make each house one of a kind. As a result, the typical home costs $154,000, well above the national average.

Newcomers often become involved in the community through the Volunteer Center of Yavapai County, which steers people to programs with different local agencies. The Sharlot Hall Museum, for example, enlists volunteers to greet and guide visitors through exhibits on the town's first settlers. The local college, Yavapai, offers senior citizens hundreds of courses, including challenging classes in genealogy and environmental chemistry, for about $35 each. The college also conducts weeklong trips through the Elderhostel Network. The most popular are a houseboat excursion on Lake Powell, 225 miles to the northeast, and a 200-mile trip to explore the Hopi Reservation, also in Arizona's northeast corner.

Fairhope, Alabama. Newcomers are heartily welcomed to this balmy town (population 9,000), where flowers bloom in window boxes year round and crime is practically nonexistent. Located on the eastern shore of Mobile Bay, Fairhope is a congenial and lively community in a splendid setting. Majestic live oaks line the streets, and Spanish moss hangs languidly from the telephone wires. While the humidity can reach an oppressive 90% or more in the summer, the average temperature is only about 60° in winter. Many homes have a view of the placid bay, and the town pier serves as a local gathering spot. One of the first communities in

Top Spots for Retiring in Style

MONEY'S board of experts. These specialists helped us determine the top places to retire: Peter Dickinson, author of *Sunbelt Retirement*; Norman Ford, author of *The 50 Healthiest Places to Live and Retire in the United States*; Alan Fox, publisher of *Where to Retire* magazine (713-974-6903); John Howells, author of *Where to Retire*; Saralee Rosenberg, co-author of *50 Fabulous Places to Retire in America*; David Savageau, author of *Retirement Places Rated*; and Robert Tillman, producer of the *Retirement in America* video series (for details, call 800-755-6555).

City and chamber of commerce phone number	Population	% of population over 65[1]	Nearest big city (miles away)	Cost of living vs. the national average[2]	Highest state income tax rate	Sunny days per year
1. Prescott, Ariz. 602-445-2000	28,211	22.5%	Phoenix (90)	+6%	7% over $300,000[3]	300
2. Fairhope, Ala. 205-928-6387	9,000	23.3	Mobile (20)	0 to –5%	5% over $6,000[4]	219
3. Mount Dora, Fla. 904-383-2165	7,500	27	Orlando (25)	0 to –6%	No income tax	238
4. Las Vegas 702-735-1616	920,000	13	Phoenix (180)	+5%	No income tax	293
5. Chapel Hill, N.C. 919-967-7075	41,524	13	Durham (8)	+4%	7.75% over $100,000[5]	217
6. Naples, Fla. 813-262-6141	19,505	29	Fort Myers (30)	+1% to +11%	No income tax	267
7. Sedona, Ariz. 602-282-7722	7,898	32	Flagstaff (27)	+6% to +11%	7% over $300,000[3]	264
8. Palm Springs, Calif. 619-325-1577	41,674	26	Los Angeles (110)	+19%	11% over $424,760[6]	313
9. Aiken, S.C. 803-641-1111	20,534	16	Augusta (20)	+1%	7% over $10,800[7]	218
10. Fayetteville, Ark. 501-521-1710	42,962	10	Tulsa (115)	–9%	7% over $25,000[8]	218
11. Kerrville, Texas 210-896-1155	18,068	30	San Antonio (60)	–6%	No income tax	224
12. Brevard, N.C. 800-648-4523	5,476	19	Asheville (30)	+2% to +8%	7.75% over $100,000[5]	218

[1]Latest available figure from U.S. Census Bureau data or the area's local chamber of commerce. [2]Range is given to approximate the cost of living when the actual figure is unavailable. From ACCRA, the American Chamber of Commerce Researchers Association. [3]Arizona allows a deduction of up to $8,400 for all residents 65 or older. [4]Alabama exempts pensions. [5]North Carolina excludes up to $4,000 of pension

| Two-bedroom house or condominium | | | |
Average monthly rent	Average cost	Average property tax	Special features
$800	$115,000	$1,000	Four museums; three performing arts facilities; outdoor sports in 15-square-mile Granite Mountain wilderness area
$400- $600	$80,000	$300- $400	Adult Recreation Center organizes dances, bridge games and social events.
$400- $600	$65,000- $70,000	$900- $1,000	Boating, sailing and other water activities are available on six-mile-long Lake Dora.
$875- $1,150	$110,000- $115,000	$640- $670	Opera, dance, symphony and major sports events; 197 gambling casinos draw top entertainment ranging from Frank Sinatra to the Bolshoi Ballet.
$800- $900	$100,000- $180,000	$1,000- $1,500	University of North Carolina at Chapel Hill has a major sports center, an art museum and a planetarium.
$1,100	$80,000 (condo)	$650	Forty golf courses; seven miles of beaches and shoreline with prime fishing, sailing and snorkeling; Philharmonic Center for the Arts attracts world-class talent.
$1,150- $1,350	$150,000- $200,000	$1,000- $1,500	Picturesque Coconino National Forest; acclaimed art galleries
$850- $900	$92,000- $103,200 (condo)	$1,100- $1,300	Door-to-door senior citizens bus service; 82 golf courses; McCallum Theater features top national tours.
$400- $850	$40,000- $85,000	$500	Horse racing, polo, symphony, dance and theater
$500	$60,000	$375	Theater, art exhibits, sports events and continuing education at the University of Arkansas
$750	$60,000- $80,000	$1,000	Cowboy Artists of America museum and major touring entertainment
$350- $500	$68,000- $95,000	$513	Pisgah National Forest has 200 miles of trout-fishing streams and 300 miles of hiking trails; Brevard Music Center attracts world-class musicians.

income for retired residents and gives credit for the elderly, based on income. [6]California gives all residents 65 or older a $64 tax credit. [7]South Carolina exempts $10,000 of pension income for all residents 65 or older. [8]Arkansas excludes the first $6,000 of pension income for residents or gives nonpensioned residents 65 or older up to $60 tax credit.

Alabama to put a horticulturist on the city payroll, Fairhope is lush with flora and flower baskets that adorn streetlights and telephone poles. Each year 200 to 250 new trees are planted along city streets and in parks.

Unlike many small, century-old communities, Fairhope welcomes newcomers. "We have a saying here," says Mayor James Nix. "If you've been here a year, you're already a native." Perhaps that is why so many retirees have settled here; some 23% of the population is over 65. Many artists and writers are also drawn to Fairhope's open-minded community. Fannie Flagg wrote her bestselling novel, *Fried Green Tomatoes at the Whistle Stop Cafe*, here. The Eastern Shore Arts Center draws on residents to teach classes in pottery, figure drawing and painting. And for more than 42 years, Fairhope has been home to an arts and crafts festival that attracts more than 450 exhibitors.

You can quickly become immersed in the community by joining the 1,200-member Adult Recreation Center ($10 a year), which has a daily roster of activities that range from video exercise classes to bridge. The center's Big Band dances attract folks from as far away as Mobile and Pensacola, Fla. If you're travel-minded, you can join the ambitious Baldwin Senior Travelers, which organizes trips to places as far away as New York City and San Juan, Puerto Rico. And the town has three scenic golf courses.

James, 73, and Evelyn Robb, 72, who moved here from Florida's West Palm Beach area, found relief in Fairhope's friendly residents and safe streets. "What you hear in the news about crime in southern Florida is just a fraction of what goes on," says James. "Five women we knew were mugged over the past few years, and burglaries were common." Home prices range from $75,000 for two-bedroom bungalows to $500,000 for a bayside house with three or four well-appointed bedrooms. The Robbs built a 1,850-square-foot house for about $150,000 in Homestead, a planned community for people who are over 55, with its own village square, medical center, fitness club, and bed-and-breakfast inn.

Fairhope has an excellent medical facility, Thomas Hospital, with 56 doctors including specialists in neurology and orthopedic surgery. Evidence of Fairhope's civic-minded citizens can be found among Thomas' volunteer staff of 300, the largest of any hospital in the state.

Mount Dora, Florida. Less than an hour from congested Orlando, this community has small-town serenity (population 7,500) and a ready supply of fairly low-cost homes. Mount Dora may shatter many of your preconceived notions of Florida. Unlike most of the tabletop-flat state, the town sits on a small hillside above six-mile-long Lake Dora. It has a historic downtown area with many landmark buildings, including the century-old Donnelly house, an exquisitely detailed steamboat gothic building that looks more like New Orleans than central Florida. Numerous small shops with attentive merchants and leafy parks add to Mount Dora's quaint, hometown feel. Ask newcomers why they settled here, and they'll invariably get dreamy-eyed and say the town reminded them of where they grew up or where they would have liked to have grown up.

Mount Dora bustles with activities. From October through April there are major events such as a bicycle festival, an antique boat show, a sailing regatta and, most notably, an annual arts festival in February that draws 200,000 visitors. No wonder the town is called Festival City. The Lawn Bowling Association, with more than 300 avid members, plays host to local and regional tournaments. You have a choice of eight movies within a nine-mile radius. Mount Dora has its own resident theater company, the Ice House Players, which stages three to four productions a year.

If you like water sports, you can sail, fish or water ski on Lake Dora or on many of the 1,400 other nearby lakes. Serious boaters can navigate a series of canals from Lake Dora 175 miles to the Atlantic Ocean via the St. Johns River. Nearby, the 182-bed Florida Hospital Waterman in Eustis has a new emergency room and can provide helicopter service to the hospital's main facility in Orlando, which has one of the best cardiac care units in the state. The cost of living in Mount Dora is comfortably below the national average. Floridians pay no state income taxes, and the first $25,000 of property value is exempt from taxation. Varied housing styles include Spanish, colonial and Victorian plus 1920s cracker-style homes with wraparound porches and tin roofs. Small homes start at $50,000, with prices rising to a range of $200,000 to $300,000 for a three-bedroom house on the lake. "It's still a buyer's market here," says Bill Casey, a local real estate broker. Nearly one dozen new residents that we interviewed agree.

Las Vegas, Nevada. Perpetual sunshine and no state income or inheritance taxes have made this seemingly sin city (population 920,000) a mecca for retirees. No longer a neon-lit strip of casinos with the nation's highest rate of serious crimes, Las Vegas is becoming almost wholesome. The crime rate is rapidly falling as the population is exploding. Low taxes and an arid climate with 293 sunny days a year have lured a monthly average of 1,000 to 2,000 new residents over age 55 to Vegas since 1990. About 40% of them are Californians fleeing economic stagnation and a collapsed real estate market. Thanks to the thriving gaming and entertainment industry, which contributes 33% of Nevada's revenues, residents pay no state income tax. And property taxes are among the country's lowest.

Residential construction is booming to house the newcomers. Most new homes, which cost as little as $50,000 for a two-bedroom condominium, are located in self-sufficient, planned communities with tennis courts, swimming pools and often shopping centers and libraries. One of the most popular, 22,000-acre Summerlin on a hill overlooking Vegas, includes Del Webb Sun City, a subdivision of 7,500 people over 55. Its stucco homes, most with desert landscaping, cost $91,500 to $240,000 and up. Residents have access to two golf courses, an indoor and outdoor swimming pool, and two recreation centers. "It's one of the most successful communities for seniors I've ever seen," says Robert Tillman, one of the members of our panel.

In eclectic Las Vegas you can enjoy the scene on the strip—the slot machines, dazzling floor shows and appetizing $4 buffets at the casinos. Or you can ignore the action and explore the natural attractions of 110-mile-long Lake Mead, just an hour's drive from the city, or 9,500-foot Mount Charleston, an hour to the north. In Las Vegas itself there are 20 golf courses, and more are planned. McCarran International Airport, a mere five minutes from the major casinos, has direct service to most major U.S. cities. Las Vegas has seven hospitals and 14 centers for urgent care, where you can drop in without an appointment for treatment of anything from a sprained ankle to strep throat. The basic cost for a visit is typically $55, although you may have to wait 30 minutes to see a doctor.

Prosperity has its price. Residents often must endure congested roads. While the crime rate has dropped from highest in the nation in 1979 to 80th lately, it still ranks among the worst third of cities surveyed by the Federal Bureau of Investigation. And the dry, sunny days may keep your spirits high in the winter. But be prepared for temperatures that can soar to 105° in July. Locals simply shrug and say, "That's what air conditioning is for."

Chapel Hill, North Carolina. When Pat, 64, and Bob Goetz, 66, of Ridgewood, N.J. began searching for a place to retire, they considered only university towns. Says Pat: "We wanted a stimulating community where we could hear jazz concerts and take crafts classes." After looking at two towns, they chose Chapel Hill, home of the University of North Carolina, mainly because of the gentle four-season climate, numerous cultural and educational activities and top-rated medical care. Chapel Hill (population 41,500) is one corner of the University Triangle, which also includes Raleigh, 20 miles east, where North Carolina State is located, and Durham, eight miles to the north, home of Duke. To share the intellectual stimulation, senior citizens can take free classes at UNC. Or they can become members of the Duke Institute for Learning and Retirement, where $65 entitles them to one class a semester or $110 gives them access to as many as five.

Each month, Chapel Hill boasts more than 50 cultural activities, half of them free, including theater productions and jazz and blues concerts. The city has a wide selection of sporting events too, but you may have to pay scalper's prices to see UNC's basketball team, 1993's national champions. Outdoors enthusiasts can hike through rolling hills and dense forests or drive three hours to the foothills of the Blue Ridge Mountains or two hours to the North Carolina beaches. For longer trips, there are lots of daily flights via Raleigh/Durham Airport, which is located 20 minutes from Chapel Hill. With 10 doctors for every 1,000 residents, four times the national average, Chapel Hill provides some of the country's best medical care. First, there's the 665-bed UNC Hospitals, with an excellent arthritis center. In Durham, the 1,125-bed Duke University Medical Center has highly esteemed cancer, heart and eye treatment.

One drawback is Chapel Hill's expensive and tight housing market. Real estate agents recommend that house hunters allow at least two months to find their ideal home. The supply is diverse, ranging from stately Victorians near the university to converted condos on the edge of town. Most homes cost around $200,000 to $300,000, but smaller two- to three-bedroom new houses and condos can be found for $100,000 or so. For more space at slightly less money, try neighboring towns. Pat and Bob Goetz settled just 10 minutes from Chapel Hill in Fearrington Village, where most of the residents are also retired. The planned community adds 50 mostly three-bedroom homes a year for $180,000 to $250,000. The village also offers a swimming pool and courts for tennis, bocci and croquet. Probably the most satisfying attractions for Pat, however, are the 100 acres of undeveloped open space. Fearrington was built on a former dairy farm and still has a hungry herd of belted Galloway cows that graze on the communal lawn.

6

Blunt the Tax Man's Big Bite

*T*here's no reason to wait patiently for the Republican leadership in Congress to get its tax-trimming and budget-reduction acts together. In this chapter, we offer retirement-related ways to cut your income taxes this year and beyond plus advice on likely changes in the law. We also show you which states currently levy the least and how to minimize the tax bills on your investment portfolio and future retirement check. As the tax landscape shifts over the next few years, sound planning will become even more important. Begin with the tips below that apply directly to retirement.

Start funding an IRA. Individual Retirement Accounts offer tremendous advantages to younger savers. You get to deduct a full $2,000 annual contribution as long as your adjusted gross income is $25,000 or less if you're single, $40,000 or less if you are married and file jointly. (AGI is your total income minus a few tax-favored items, such as alimony you pay. Taxable income, the amount on which your tax rate is based, is your AGI minus your deductions and exemptions.) If your spouse works, you can each contribute $2,000 to your respective IRAs. What's more, odds are strong that Congress will pass a "back-end" IRA soon. This would permit nondeductible annual contributions of up to $4,000 per couple ($2,000 for singles). Like a traditional IRA, the earnings would grow tax deferred. Then after five years you could make withdrawals tax-free if you used the money for retirement, a first-home purchase, college or large medical expenses. The Republican proposal would even let you convert all or part of your current IRA to a back-end account, not including rollovers from employer-sponsored plans. To do so, you would have to pay income tax on the previously untaxed portion of the IRA, although you could spread the tax over four years. For now, however, you're better off with a deductible IRA. Later you can convert to a back-end account if you need the money.

Exploit your state's breaks. The IRS estimates that nearly 8 million Americans overpaid their state and local tax bills because they didn't realize they were eligible for special breaks. To learn about such goodies, curl up with the instruction booklet for your state tax return. You'll be the richer for spending time with it. For example, if you're retired and collecting Social Security benefits, they won't be taxed in Alabama, Arizona, Arkansas, California, Delaware, Georgia, Hawaii, Idaho, Illinois, Indiana, Kentucky, Louisiana, Maine, Maryland, Massachusetts, Michigan, Mississippi, New Jersey, New York, North Carolina, Ohio, Oklahoma, Oregon, Pennsylvania, South Carolina, Virginia and the District of Columbia. And at least part of a retiree's pension is exempt from taxes in Alabama, Arkansas, Colorado, Delaware, Georgia, Hawaii, Illinois, Louisiana, Maryland, Michigan, Mississippi, Montana, New Jersey, New Mexico, New York, North Carolina, Oregon, Pennsylvania, South Carolina and Utah.

Defend your lower-tax abode. Watch out if you own dwellings in two states and work part of the time in the state with the higher taxes. In recent years, California, New York and other high-tax states have begun taxing the entire income of such residents including interest, dividends and capital gains earned in other states. What to do? First, find out what constitutes taxable residency in each state where you work or own property. Most states won't consider you a resident unless you spend more than half the year at a home within their borders. But New York and other voracious

Avoid Those Onerous IRA Penalties

The IRS penalizes over a million people annually for taking money out of their IRAs too early—or too late. Folks who withdrew money before age 59.5 had to pay a 10% penalty on top of ordinary income taxes. Those who didn't start taking out money by 70.5 paid 50% of the amount that they should have withdrawn. Both of these stiff tax blows, however, can be avoided by heeding the following advice.

▶ **Early withdrawals.** To tap your IRA without penalty before 59.5, you must make annual withdrawals that could conceivably last for the rest of your life. To calculate the appropriate amounts, first obtain an IRS life expectancy table (call 800-829-3676 and request Form 590). Then divide the value of your IRA by the number of years the table indicates you may live. For example, a 52-year-old with a $500,000 IRA can anticipate sticking around another 31 years. So he or she would have to withdraw approximately $16,000 a year. You must continue to take this amount annually for five years or until you turn 59.5, whichever is later. Before starting withdrawals, be sure you require that much money. If you need, say, $10,000 this year, that's an extra $40,000 you must take out of the account in the subsequent years. Thus a big chunk of your savings won't grow tax-deferred.

▶ **Late withdrawals.** You can defer these until age 70.5. After that you must take out an IRS-approved minimum amount each year. To calculate it, you have to divide your IRA balance by your life expectancy. If you don't want to take that much, write to the financial services company holding your IRA and designate a beneficiary. You may then calculate the minimum withdrawal using your joint life expectancies listed in the IRS table. For example, a 71-year-old woman has a single life expectancy of around 15 years. If she has accumulated a $500,000 IRA, she must take out at least $32,680 a year. But if she includes her 61-year-old husband in the calculation, their joint life expectancy of 25 years would reduce the minimum to $19,763.

▶ **What if you die first?** Then your spouse or other beneficiary can roll over the IRA into his or her own account, name a child or grandchild as a new beneficiary and recalculate the minimum withdrawal. The IRS insists that the child's age, for purposes of the calculation, be figured as no more than 10 years less than your beneficiary's age. So if your spouse is 70 and the grandchild is 15, the minimum must be computed as if the child were 60. When the child inherits the IRA, the minimum could be recalculated again, using his or her actual life expectancy.

states may try to tax your entire income if you spend as little as one month within their borders. How can you document that your home in the low-tax state is your main residence? Keep records that show where you spend most of your time, such as phone and electricity bills. Also keep documents showing where you go to church, register your car and vote.

Set up a defined-benefit Keogh. If you're 45 or older and generate income from self-employment, investigate this potential monster of a tax shelter. Like other defined-benefit pensions, this special type of Keogh is based on your life expectancy plus the amount you want to draw down as an annuity when you retire. The maximum benefit you can receive is your average income over your three top earning years or $120,000, whichever is less. Hiring an actuary to administer such a plan isn't cheap (up to $3,000 to set one up plus around $1,250 a year). You have until year-end to open a Keogh, though you can fund the plan through the April 15 filing deadline.

Seek out a rabbi trust. Many companies now offer their highly paid executives so-called rabbi trusts (because the method was first used by a congregation for its rabbi). Your employer sets up an irrevocable trust, stashes money in it every year for you and pays the income tax on the fund. You then have retirement dollars building up to be spent when you are presumably in a lower tax bracket. One drawback is that you have no control over your trust, which can even be seized by creditors to pay your employer's debts. So be confident about your company's long-term health before asking for the rabbi's blessing.

▶ Defend Your Retirement Check

It's a frightening thought. You're ready to grab the retirement money you built up over your 25-year career, and you suddenly realize that this could be the largest single amount you'll ever see. When a lump-sum pension, 401(k) and other corporate savings plans are totted up, workers can walk away with $1 million or more. Thus your first task is to keep as much of it as possible from the IRS. But beware that your distribution has a short fuse. If you fritter away more than 60 days after receiving the money before deciding what to do with it, the amount may be subject to a 10% penalty as well as federal tax.

You have two ways to ease the blow. You can take the money and use a tax-cutting technique called special averaging. Or you can roll over your payout into an IRA and postpone paying the tax until you withdraw the money, presumably when you'll be in a lower tax bracket than you are now. Which method is better depends mostly on the size of your settlement and how long you have until you stop working altogether. Before making a choice, you need to understand the main points of both approaches.

Average over five or 10 years. You may qualify for either five- or 10-year averaging, depending on your age. Both can yield after-tax results that are far more favorable than paying up in a single year. As the name suggests, this legerdemain computes your tax as if you received the distribution over a five- or 10-year period. There are entry rules, however. To use averaging, your lump-sum distribution must meet the following four requirements. It must be:

▶ A qualified pension, profit-sharing or Keogh plan in which you participated at least five years. Your plan administrator can tell you whether the plan qualifies.

▶ The entire balance that is due to you from all of your employer's qualified retirement plans.

▶ Paid to you within a single tax year. If you retire this year and pay taxes on a calendar-year basis, you must receive your entire balance by December 31.

▶ Paid after you turn 59.5. The age test doesn't apply, however, if you were born before January 1, 1936.

How to figure the tax. If you meet all those tests, you can apply averaging to the taxable portion of your lump-sum distribution. This includes your employer's contributions to your account and its earnings over the years—but not your own nondeductible contributions. The taxable amount is listed on the Form 1099-R that you will receive from your employer. If your distribution is less than $70,000, part of it is absolutely tax-free thanks to the minimum-distribution allowance. This break exempts 50% of the first $20,000 of a lump-sum distribution from tax. As the payout rises above $20,000, however, the tax-free portion phases out. At $30,000, $8,000 is tax-free. At $40,000, it's $6,000. At $50,000, it's $4,000. At $60,000, it's $2,000. And at $70,000 or more, it's zero.

The tax on the rest of the distribution is figured using grade school math. First, you divide the remaining distribution by five. Next, find the tax on the result using the rates for single taxpayers; the rates are listed in the IRS instruction booklet for filing your annual tax return. Finally, multiply that tax by five. Let's say you receive a lump-sum distribution of $180,000 that includes no nondeductible contributions by you. The payout is too big to benefit from the minimum-distribution allowance, so the entire amount will be taxable. Using five-year averaging, one-fifth of $180,000 is $36,000. Tax on that amount is about $7,214. Multiplying $7,214 by five gives you a tax bill of $36,070. Without using averaging, the tax could run as high as $71,280 (39.6% of $180,000).

If you were born before 1936, you may use 10-year averaging, which works the same way as its five-year cousin except that you divide and multiply by 10 instead of five. There's one catch, however: With 10-year averaging, you must use the higher and more steeply graduated 1986 tax rates for singles, which ranged from 11% to 50%.

If you qualify to average over five or 10 years, use Form 4972 to figure your tax both ways and choose the one that results in the lower bill. You might also compare it with what your tax would be if you didn't use averaging. If the difference is small and you don't plan to quit working altogether, you might want to pay the regular tax. The reason is that you can use averaging only once. If you expect a bigger lump-sum distribution from another qualified plan in the future, you might postpone taking advantage of averaging until you retire for good. Your tax can be even lower if you were born before January 1, 1936 and earned retirement benefits before 1974. In that case, you may treat part of the payout as a capital gain and pay a flat 20% tax on it. That can be a bargain compared with current income tax rates of up to 39.6% and the top capital-gains rate of 28%. Your employer will tell you how much qualifies.

The case for tax-free rollovers. To postpone taxes on your lump sum, you can roll it over into an IRA and let the money grow tax deferred until you withdraw it. If you wish, you can stash the distribution in two or more IRAs, for example, putting part in a stock fund and the rest in a bond fund. If you have a Keogh retirement plan set up with self-employment earnings, you can fend off the IRS with a rollover and keep your averaging over five or 10 years. Invest your company-plan distribution in the Keogh. Then, if you later take a lump-sum distribution from it, you can use averaging to figure the tax.

The basic rollover rules are simple. It must be completed within 60 days of receiving the distribution. The money can then be placed in a new or existing IRA. If your lump sum is paid in installments over the calendar year, the 60-day rule applies to each of the payments. If you are unlucky enough to miss the deadline, you'll owe tax on all the money plus a 10% penalty if you're under age 59.5. Once made, the rollover can't be revoked. Ask your employer to transfer the money directly to the IRA of your choice. If you make the rollover yourself, 20% of the payout will be withheld under IRS rules, and you will have to claim a credit on your next tax return to get it back. Worse, if you're under 59.5, you'll have to pay the nonrefundable 10% early-withdrawal penalty on the 20% unless you make it up out of your own pocket. Don't include your after-tax contributions to the plan or lump-sum severance pay in the rollover. If you do, the IRS will levy a 6% excise tax on the excess amount.

Keep in mind that you don't have to roll over your entire distribution. You can take some of the money and pay tax on it plus a 10% penalty if you're under 59.5. (In this case, however, you can't use averaging.) The amount rolled over will still escape taxes until withdrawn from your IRA. You must report a rollover on line 16 of your 1040 but only for information purposes. If not, the IRS will assume you're omitting income and send you a bill for additional tax.

Which method is better? Don't rush into either one blindly. Remember too that a rollover merely postpones the tax man's inevitable payday. In fact, if you are in a higher tax bracket when you withdraw the money, a rollover could actually wind up costing you more than simply paying your tax when you take your distribution. Before electing a rollover, have your tax pro or financial planner compute the current tax on your lump-sum distribution using one or more of the methods described earlier. Compare this amount to an estimate of the tax you'll pay on future distributions from an IRA. Make sure your pro takes into account the money you'll earn in the IRA.

Chances are the rollover will win hands down. Consider a new retiree who at 62 receives $250,000 from his company's 401(k) at the start of this year. He plans to let the money grow at 6.5% annually in an IRA until 72 and then withdraw the money gradually over the next 15 years. He expects to be in the combined 34% federal and state bracket during those years. Thus his best bet is clearly a rollover. The $250,000, undiminished by taxes, will grow to $440,643 by the time he turns 72. By contrast, with 10-year averaging, his after-tax $205,882 (his $250,000 payout minus an immediate tax of $44,118) will increase to just $300,471 at 72. By choosing a rollover, you'll avoid the 15% tax penalty on what the government deems to be excess annual distributions from a retirement plan—$148,500 at last count. (The amount rises each year with inflation.) You alternatively can take an amount that doesn't exceed the excise tax limit and shield the rest in an IRA. Of course, you may need all the money immediately. In that case, you should pay the tax using averaging and be assured that you've done all you can to shield your precious lump from tax meltdown.

▶ Keep More of Your Portfolio's Profit

The best news for many aspiring retirees is the probability of a sizable tax cut on capital gains. That's the profit you clear when you sell an investment that has risen in value as opposed to the dividends or interest you collect along the way. Better yet, the favorable tax treatment accorded such gains, which heretofore has solely benefited people with high incomes, may soon be available to all taxpayers, regardless of income.

Under federal tax law, you pay no more than 28% on gains from investments held for at least a year. That's a good deal less than the tax on your income if you are in the 31%, 36% or 39.6% brackets. (If you're in the 15% or 28% bracket, your gains tax is the same as your regular marginal tax rate.) But the Republican leaders who have taken over Congress want to cut the tax on long-term capital gains to half of an investor's top income tax rate. That means people in the 39.6% bracket (at last count, taxable earnings above $256,500) would cede only 19.8% of their gains to Uncle Sam. Those in the lowest 15% bracket, including many teenagers and retirees, would pay a super-low 7.5%.

Here are the tax basics of various investments. In each case, we point to the most tax-efficient choices and show the steps you can take now to lighten the tax burden on your profits. The advice is important because

How to Figure All Your Capital Gains

To compute a gain or loss when you sell a stock or mutual fund, take the proceeds of the sale and subtract your basis—or cost of acquiring the shares. Sounds simple. But the tax code can make it tricky depending on how you obtained the stock. Follow these general rules.

IF YOU GOT STOCK BY...	...YOUR BASIS IS
Buying it directly	The price you paid for the shares plus any fees or commissions you paid to buy them. Fees or commissions on the sale do not add to your basis but can be subtracted from the proceeds, thus also reducing your gain.
A dividend reinvestment plan (DRIP)	The full market value of the stock on the date the dividend was paid plus any fees or commissions even if, as is often the case, the DRIP lets you buy shares at a discount.
Receiving it as a gift	The donor's original basis plus any gift tax the donor has to pay. Exception: if you later sell the stock for a loss, your basis is the lesser of the donor's basis or the stock's fair market value on the date the gift was given.
Inheriting it	The market value of the shares on the date you inherited them. This often is the same as the donor's date of death. But in some cases the executor may choose an "alternate valuation date." To check, ask the executor or review the estate tax return. Note that even if you sell the stock within a year, any profit is considered a long-term rather than a short-term capital gain because the stock was inherited.
Receiving it after a stock split	The same, for your total stake, as it was before the split. To find out your new per-share basis, take the original basis of your holding and divide it by the number of shares you own after the split became effective.
Obtaining it as a stock dividend	Whatever the company tells you it is. How's that? Sometimes a company issues a dividend in the form of stock or spins off part of its business and gives shareholders stock in the new firm. You usually won't owe any tax on this so-called stock distribution even if it came as a dividend. But the per-share basis of your holding will be reduced by a percentage that the company will calculate and report to you.
Exercising a stock option	The price you paid for the shares (plus fees or commissions) even though it is lower than the market value at the time of purchase. You must retain the shares for at least a year after buying them, and for two years after receiving the option, or else any profit from their sale will be taxed as ordinary income rather than capital gains.

taxes take a bigger toll on investments than most people realize. Taxation at today's rates would have zapped from 7% to 37% of the total return of assorted stock, bond and real estate holdings over the past 10 years. "Income taxes are at their highest since 1982," observes John Bogle, chairman of the Vanguard family of mutual funds. "So the risks investors face are the same as ever, but their potential returns are lower."

The tax code is filled with quirks that let you defer, reduce or even avoid taxes. To postpone the tax bite, you can concentrate on growth investments, where the profit comes mostly from price appreciation (taxable when you sell) rather than current income (taxed in the year you collect it). You can further reduce taxes by timing your sales, especially of losers. And you can avoid taxes altogether by choosing the right kinds of bonds or, if you own real estate, by swapping your old property for new property to duck the tax that would ordinarily be due. The message here is to be smart about taxes, not fanatical. While it is important to reduce investment taxes, that should not be your only goal. Go for the most promising investment. Use what you learn here to make sure that it will still be the most rewarding choice after you pay the taxes.

How to shield your stocks. It's not what you earn as an investor that counts; it's what you keep after the taxman takes his cut. Growth stocks, which deliver most of their return through price gains, enjoy a major tax advantage over income stocks, which pay high dividends. Not only are price gains subject to a maximum levy of 28%, vs. 39.6% for dividends, but the tax isn't due until you cash out, leaving more of your money invested. Here are MONEY's tax-savvy tips for investing in stock. The first three apply only to people in at least the 31% bracket (which lately started at $56,551 for singles and $94,251 for couples), though they may work for everyone if Congress cuts the tax on long-term capital gains sufficiently. The remaining points generally apply to all investors.

▶ **Go for growth in taxable portfolios.** Keeping a growth stock in an IRA or Keogh is like buying a Ferrari to drive to your commuter bus stop. You don't really need the account's tax protection because growth stocks derive 90% of their return from price increase, which isn't taxed until you sell. You also forgo the right to use any losses you incur to offset gains or ordinary income. When you finally withdraw your earnings from the account, you'll pay tax at the rates for ordinary income (which run as high as 39.6%) rather than at the maximum 28% capital-gains rate.

▶ **Seek income in tax-deferred accounts.** Your IRA, Keogh and the like provide a comfy home for high-dividend stocks whose payouts would be taxed each year. Good candidates include utility stocks (they generally pay 6% to 7% a year in dividends), financial services firms (2% to 4%) and many blue chips.

▶ **Shoot for long-term price gains.** The favorable tax treatment of capital gains applies only to assets held at least a year. If you cash out sooner, you'll pay your marginal income tax rate. So unless you've got hold of a real rocket—say, a stock that doubled in eight months but now seems headed for a fall—stay invested for at least 12 months before ejecting.

▶ **Sell your priciest shares first.** Let's suppose that you have bought a company's shares at various prices over the years and now want to unload some for a profit. Since the tax code lets you designate which shares you sell, dump the ones that cost you the most in order to hold down your capital gains. Sure, you'll pay tax on those gains someday. In general, however, it's better to pay tax in the future rather than today.

▶ **Donate stocks to good causes.** The next time you want to be generous to a tax-exempt group, give away appreciated stock instead of cash. Why? Imagine that you bought a stock for $5,000 a decade ago and that it's now worth $15,000. If you cash out, you'll owe tax of

When Should You Take Social Security?

That's the No. 1 question for many retirees. Fully 62% of men and 73% of women begin at 62 even though they get only 80% of the benefits they would be due if they waited until 65. Whether you should follow the crowd depends on your financial circumstances, your plans for working in retirement and your willingness to gamble on your longevity. At 62, a man can expect to live for another 18 years, a woman for 22 years. Here are your options.

▶ **Start early.** The rule of thumb is that you should consider collecting your first check at 62 if Social Security benefits will amount to less than 50% of your retirement income, or if your net worth, excluding your home, is more than $100,000. That way, you can enjoy the extra income in your early retirement years and still have plenty of assets for your later years. Here's why. Let's assume you're eligible for an annual Social Security benefit of $12,000 at 65. If you file for it at 62, you'll get only $9,600 a year. Even so, by 65, you will have pocketed a total of $28,800. You won't reach the break-even point until 74 (when the total of all your Social Security checks will be the same as if you had waited to file for benefits at 65). If you can afford to invest your Social Security checks, you can extend the break-even point even farther.

▶ **Wait until 65 or even later.** You probably should postpone collecting benefits until you can get bigger checks at 65 if Social Security will provide 50% or more of your retirement income, or if your net worth, excluding your home, is less than $100,000. The life expectancy of a male or female is greater than the break-even point. So if you base your decision on the odds, you're better off waiting until 65. If you put off collecting benefits beyond 65, you will be rewarded with even bigger checks. But the actuarial odds generally favor people who begin cashing in at 65. Postponing benefits is the only sensible decision when you hold a job in retirement that pays more than $8,160 a year (if you're between 62 and 65) or $11,280 (between 65 and 70). The amount rises yearly with inflation. When earnings top these limits, the government will cut your benefits $1 for every $2 of excess pay from age 62 to 65 and $1 for every $3 between the ages of 65 and 70. Once you turn 70, however, you'll receive a full benefit regardless of how much you earn. Of course, you'll have to continue paying FICA tax on your earnings even while Social Security is paying you.

up to 28% (or $2,800) on that $10,000 gain. But if you give the stock to charity, the organization pockets the full $15,000 value because it doesn't have to pay tax on capital gains. And you get to take the same $15,000 tax deduction that you would have taken if you'd donated cash instead of stock even though your shares are worth only $12,200 to you after taxes.

▶ **Time losses to claim a tax prize.** Every investor winds up holding losing cards. But at least you can deduct the damage outside of a tax-sheltered account. You are allowed to write off capital losses against the full amount of any gains you may reap during the year, and then against as much as $3,000 more of ordinary income. And don't worry if you can't write off the entire loss in one year. You can carry leftover losses forward to future years until they are all used up.

▶ **Avoid these tax tangles.** Watch out for the wash sale rule that prohibits you from deducting a loss on the sale of a stock if you buy any shares of the same com- pany within 30 days either before or after that sale. Take into account the commission you paid when you bought a stock, as well as that imposed when you sold it, when figuring your gain or loss. And be sure to claim a U.S. tax credit if foreign tax was withheld from divi- dends paid to you by an international stock.

How to tame fund taxes. Many mutual fund investors are jolted when they discover they owe tax on a fund that lost money in a given year. Sound impossi- ble? Not at all. It happens because a fund must distrib- ute to shareholders nearly all the yearly income it earned from dividends and interest, plus any net gains it realized from selling securities, even if it had a losing year. Don't get irate, get informed. Start by employing the following mutual fund tax tips.

▶ **Favor low turnover and tax savvy.** Funds that fol- low a buy-and-hold strategy tend to realize fewer capital gains than those that trade actively. So if you are choosing between two funds with otherwise similar performance, go for the one with the lower turnover ratio (the proportion of its assets that have been bought or sold within the past year). You can find the ratio by calling a fund or by looking in its semiannual report. Low turnover is not the only positive indicator. A tax-savvy manager can be an active trader and still hold the tax bite down by timing any losses to offset the fund's gains. When considering a hot fund that has a high turnover ratio, check out its tax-efficiency ratio. That's the percentage of its total return that is left after taxes are paid. After-tax fund winners tend to have tax-efficiency ratios of around 80% or better.

▶ **Go for funds that protect profits.** Several fund companies have launched carefully managed index funds that aim to deliver maximum tax efficiency by timing their losses to offset most of their gains. (Index funds are those that try to match or beat the performance of market benchmarks like the S&P 500 stock index.) Discount broker Charles Schwab has several, including International Index, Schwab 1000 and Small-Cap Index. The Vanguard fund family entries include Capital Appreciation Portfolio, Growth & Income Portfolio and Balanced Portfolio.

▶ **Invest overseas in taxable accounts.** Under tax treaties between the U.S. and foreign countries, funds that are more than half invested outside the U.S. typically have to pay 5% to 10% of whatever they earn on those holdings to the foreign governments (just as you would if you owned a foreign stock). In return, you are eligible for as much as a dollar-for-dollar reduction of your U.S. tax provided you hold the funds in a taxable account. If you park them in a tax-deferred retirement account, however, the credit is worthless.

How to shelter real estate income. Compared with other investments, property enjoys some truly remarkable tax perks. To begin with, you can deduct the interest you pay on mortgages totaling as much as $1 million on your first and second homes even if you rent out that second home part of the year. If you buy real estate strictly as an investment, you can depreciate (write off) the full price over the next 27.5 or 39 years. And if you help manage the property by, say, interviewing prospective tenants and setting rents, you can deduct any operating losses against as much as $25,000 of non-investment income. With stocks and bonds, this kind of deduction is limited to $3,000 a year. Even REITs (real estate investment trusts), which own interests in property or mortgages and trade like stocks, have certain tax advantages. If your REIT profits from the sale of a property, you pay tax on your share at the maximum long-term gains rate of 28%, not at the generally higher rate for short-term gains. That's true even if the REIT owned the asset for less than a year.

If you want to unload a highly appreciated piece of property but stay invested in real estate, you can duck capital-gains tax with a nifty maneuver that's called a "like kind exchange." Here's how one works. You, as exchanger, transfer the deed to your property to a buyer. The buyer gives his payment to an intermediary, often an attorney. You then have 45 days to identify property you want to buy and 180 days to close on it. At the closing on the second property, the intermediary pays the seller (you chip in too if the new property is worth more than the old) and the seller gives you his deed. You now own the property you want—and owe no tax on the real estate you traded away.

▶ Don't Own a Policy on Your Life

Who owns your life insurance policy? If you're like most people, the answer is you. And it may be a costly error. Why? If you own the policy, the proceeds that are paid out when you die could get whacked by estate taxes of 37% to 55%. Here are the possible tax consequences of four common ways to own life insurance policies.

▶ **Insured as owner.** At your death, the IRS will count the insurance proceeds as part of your estate. If the death benefit pushes the estate's value above $600,000, the excess is subject to federal estate tax.

▶ **Spouse as owner.** If he or she owns the policy, the proceeds won't be taxed. If your spouse names someone else as beneficiary, such as a child, the IRS considers the death benefit to be a gift. Anything above $10,000 may be subject to 37% to 55% tax.

▶ **Nonspousal beneficiary as owner.** The IRS won't consider the policy as part of your taxable estate, and the beneficiary won't owe tax on the proceeds. But watch out. If you give a policy to the beneficiary, the IRS will regard the transfer as a gift. That's not a problem with term insurance because the policy has no value until you die. With a cash-value policy such as whole life, however, you may trigger gift taxes if the cash value exceeds $10,000. If you die within three years of giving away any type of life policy, the death benefit will still be included in your taxable estate. After you've transferred your policy to the beneficiary, you may pay the premium with no tax consequences, as long as it doesn't exceed $10,000 a year.

▶ **Trust as owner.** The IRS won't count the death benefit as part of your taxable estate, and the trust's beneficiaries will get the proceeds tax-free. With a trust, you're subject to the same gift-tax limitations that apply if the beneficiary owns the policy. So why have a trust own the policy? Because you gain flexibility with a trust, which a lawyer can draw up for as little as $500. A trust can be set up to provide steady income to a beneficiary. A trust also can pay the taxes on your estate without the insurance proceeds being included among its assets. For a trust's assets to escape being included in your taxable estate, the trust must be irrevocable. That means you can't change the terms of the trust or terminate it even if your beneficiary is your spouse and you divorce.

7

Protect Your Nest Egg From Perils

*M*any people approaching retirement harbor fears of financial disaster. But you can sidestep potential pitfalls by taking a good hard look at where your net worth is most vulnerable to unexpected assaults—and why. Don't limit your soul searching to the investments and real estate that were covered earlier in this book. Your pension, if you have one, is among your most valuable retirement assets, followed by tax-deferred company savings plans, like 401(k)s, and life insurance policies with sizable cash values. Insuring against threats to your family's health and pre-retirement earning power is also critical. Whether you will wind up living the retirement of your dreams or of your nightmares may depend on how quickly you recognize and overcome the hazards discussed in this chapter. Among them:

You may not get a pension. For those lucky enough to have one, the monthly pension check can replace as much as a third of pre-retirement income. These days nearly a third of retirees collect private pensions, compared with only 9% in 1962. But if current trends continue, the heyday of the traditional pension is past. Many companies, particularly small ones, are shunning defined-benefit pensions in favor of less expensive defined-contribution plans such as 401(k)s. The number of defined-benefit plans has dropped 33% in recent years. By 1997, defined-contribution programs are expected to account for 43% of retirement assets, up from 30% a decade earlier. With a defined benefit, employees are guaranteed a fixed monthly payout for life and usually are not required to make contributions of their own. By contrast, defined contributions are funded primarily by employees, who also assume all investment risk. Thus the plan may never amount to much if you fail to contribute enough to it or if you mis-manage your investments. In short, you become even more vulnerable to other threats described below.

Medical benefits could be cut. Bills for doctors, drugs and hospitals can wreck even the best retirement plans. Employer-sponsored medical coverage is especially crucial for early retirees who are too young to qualify for Medicare, the government insurance program for those age 65 and older. But company coverage is also valuable because it covers most of the costs that Medicare doesn't. Today only a third of all retirees get free or low-cost health insurance from their former employers—and that figure is declining fast. Employers are scaling back partly because they must report the cost of future retiree health benefits on their balance sheets, thereby reducing profits. According to a survey of 2,400 firms, 7% have ended or plan to end benefits for future retirees, 30% have raised premiums for current retirees and 26% have hiked deductibles or co-payments for current retirees. Some who've suffered cutbacks have sued former employers to reinstate promised benefits. But courts so far have ruled that employers have the right to change or terminate such plans as long as documents describing employee and retiree benefits make that position clear.

Social Security shrinks more. This squeeze is underway. You now are taxed on up to 50% of your Social Security benefits if the total of your adjusted gross income, nontaxable interest, and half of your Social Security benefits exceeds $25,000 ($32,000 if you are married). If that total exceeds $34,000 ($44,000 for cou-ples), you owe tax on up to 85% of your benefits. If you keep working past 65, your benefits will rise by a certain yearly percentage until age 70. These increases range from 3% to 8% depending on the year of your birth. The age at which you can collect full Social Security benefits, now 65, is scheduled to rise to 66 in 2005 and to 67 in 2022. And experts believe Congress will keep nibbling away at Social Security. The retirement age might be further advanced, all benefits may be taxed and cost-of-living adjustments may even be scaled back or frozen for a while.

You'll sabotage yourself. Like most Americans, you represent the single most potent threat to your prosperous retirement. The danger is that you won't put enough aside or that you will squander your savings. The U.S. personal savings rate has stood at around 4% since the late 1980s, half what it was in the 1970s and a scandal compared with other nations. The Japanese save at three times our rate, the Germans double. And despite an increased tendency to retire solo, many singles spend like they expect to retire on someone else's savings. On average, married couples put away 5% of their pretax pay, single men save 3% and single women save less than 2%. More unsettling, most people tend to blow their retirement savings while they are employed. One study found that just 11% of workers who received lump-sum distributions from a tax-deferred retirement account opted to roll over the entire amount into a similar account, while 34% spent all of the payout.

▶ *Take the Pulse of Your Pension*

Each year about a hundred companies default on their pension plans, stranding both their retirees and workers who are anticipating regular pension checks at retirement. The victims typically turn to the federal PBGC (Pension Benefit Guaranty Corporation), which recently paid $721 million in annual benefits to 174,200 retirees covered by nearly 2,000 plans. The PBGC, a 20-year-old government insurance agency, gets its money both from the terminated plans' assets and from premiums paid by most companies that provide employees with traditional defined-benefit pensions.

For many retired managers, however, the PBGC replaces only part of the pension once promised by their employers. With payouts capped by law, the agency lately paid a maximum benefit of around $2,575 a month. Worse, if you took early retirement at age 55, your PBGC benefit plummets to about $1,160 even if you were due more under your former employer's pension rules. If you retired at age 62, benefits max out at $2,033. How likely is your pension to default? The agency estimates that 16,000 of the 64,000 plans it insures are underfunded. Even if your company's program isn't one of the weaklings, it may not be flush enough to keep paying benefits throughout your retirement. So, whether you're retired or still working, it's crucial to determine the odds of your pension lasting the rest of your life. If your pension looks shaky, you can at least get an early start on boosting your savings to ensure that your retirement is comfortable. Here's how to take the pulse of your pension's health.

Identify your plan's type. If you're in a defined-contribution program, such as a 401(k), you can relax as long as you're putting as much money in it as you can afford. Your benefit at retirement will depend on how much you've contributed, the amount your employer may have matched and how investments in the plan have fared over the course of time. All this is easy to track because most employers provide quarterly statements of your account's value. Since the account is your property, your company can't legally raid it to pay off its debts. Even if the firm fails, you can transfer your retirement money elsewhere or leave it with the management company that acts as your plan's trustee. That's not the case with a traditional defined-benefit pension. Many companies in shaky financial condition underfund these plans, diverting money to business expenses. That puts your retirement benefits at risk.

Be Wary of This Private Pension Spiel

Life insurance agents have come up with another novel pitch to peddle policies—use the tax-shelter benefits of your coverage to build your own private pension plan. If you salt away, say, $1,000 a month or more for 20 years into a universal or variable life policy, the salesman explains, the investment portion of the policy (called the cash value) would grow by as much as 12% a year. Then, when you need income for retirement, you could stop paying premiums, withdraw what you've paid in and begin borrowing against the policy through the insurer's free or low-cost loans, which don't have to be repaid. The outstanding loan balance and any interest would be deducted from the death benefit when you die. And the loan proceeds escape income taxes.

Sounds good. But these spiels can be dangerously misleading. The policy's return would shrink if interest rates drop or, in the case of variable life, if the stock market falls. Then your pile for retirement might never materialize. The tax-free loans could also backfire. That's because borrowing could so erode the cash value that you would have to pay more premiums just to keep the policy in force. If the policy lapses, all loans in excess of the premiums you've paid plus any remaining cash value would become taxable. So if you plowed in $12,000 a year for 20 years, then borrowed $40,000 annually for 20 years, and the policy lapsed, you would owe taxes on at least $560,000. That's a $156,800 bill for someone in the 28% federal tax bracket. Our advice? Resist the temptation of these private pensions and stash your savings in 401(k)s and IRAs.

Check its financial health. Within 90 days of becoming eligible for the plan, you automatically should receive a booklet summarizing how it operates. For specific information, however, you must ask your employee benefits office for a copy of Form 5500, which the company files each year with the U.S. Department of Labor. If you prefer, you can request the document from the department. Just send your employer's identification number (on last year's W-2 tax form) and the plan number (in the summary booklet) to the Division of Technical Assistance and Inquiries, Pension and Welfare Benefits

Administration, U.S. Department of Labor, 200 Constitution Ave. N.W., Washington, D.C. 20210. When you receive the Form 5500, pay attention to the actuary's report in the back. If the actuary expresses reservations about the plan's financial health, you have good reason to worry. Of course, even if your plan is sound today, you can't be sure it will be healthy in the future. So obtain Form 5500 every few years to check the actuary's report.

Look for PBGC life support. The agency stands behind nearly all private defined-benefit plans. The exceptions are those provided by professional service employers, such as lawyers or doctors, with fewer than 26 employees; church groups with any number of employees; and state, local and federal governments. In addition to the benefit limits described earlier, the PBGC operates under another noteworthy limitation. It steps in only in the event of total default. If your pension plan can scrape together part of your promised benefit, the PBGC won't pony up the difference. If your company can afford to pay more than the PBGC maximum but less than it had promised to pay you, the PBGC will take over the pension and pay you the maximum amount the plan can afford.

Most companies fund their pension obligations appropriately, of course. If they don't and the companies fail to correct shortfalls after repeated warnings, they risk legal action by the Department of Labor and tax penalties from the IRS that could equal as much as the amount of underfunding. Congress tightened the pressure on underfunded pensions in 1994 in part by raising insurance premiums for underfunded plans and requiring any plan less than 90% funded to alert all its beneficiaries. Even so, the PBGC figures about a quarter of companies have not yet funded their plans properly. What can you do in the event that your employer is one of them? Start by dealing with the problem the same way you would any financial setback. Try to economize so that you can get by if you're already retired or save more if you're still working. If you're employed, you should invest as much money as you can in tax-deferred retirement plans such as 401(k)s. In short, if Washington can't reform your employer, you probably can't either. So you'll have to take charge of your own retirement.

▶ *How Divorce Can Crimp Your Plans*

Even longstanding marriages can be torn apart when children move out, careers plateau, aged parents die or future options seem to dwindle. The number of divorces among people over age 55 is a third higher than 20 years ago. If your marriage breaks up, your shattered emotions may eventually heal. But your retirement plans might not after you and your ex split your assets. Just how a divorcing couple's assets are divided up can depend on the state they live in. While all courts must follow federal law in dealing with company-sponsored retirement plans, states have their own laws on splitting assets in IRAs and Keoghs. Courts in community-property states (Arizona, California, Idaho, Louisiana, Nevada, New Mexico, Texas, Washington and Wisconsin) usually require divorcing spouses to share assets in those plans equally. Other states give judges more discretion, often to the detriment of lower-paid spouses. Judges in these states generally award as much as two-thirds of the marital property to the higher wage earner. Whatever your share, it probably won't be enough to finance the retirement you've been planning. Here's how a retirement stockpile dwindles in divorce.

Defined contribution. These plans may be 401(k)s, 403(b)s or SEPs (Simplified Employee Pensions) if you're salaried, or Keoghs and SEPs if you're self-employed. You may also have an IRA. If your plans and your spouse's are roughly equal in value, the court will likely let you both keep your plans intact. Otherwise, the judge may divide the total between you, instructing your employers in a court order which share belongs to each of you. Such plans are relatively easy to split up because they consist of company stock or money invested in securities. If the court divides your 401(k) in half, most companies will set up a separate account for your spouse's share. Henceforth, your contributions will go entirely into your account. Some companies will let ex-spouses withdraw everything in their accounts as lump sums that they can roll over into IRAs or take as cash. Other companies allow withdrawals over time, as with any retirement account. Either way, the law imposes no 10% penalty on withdrawals by ex-spouses who are younger than 59.5.

Defined benefit. To make things simple, many divorcing couples agree to let one spouse keep the traditional pension, while the other takes all or a portion of the 401(k)s and other defined-contribution accounts. If you must split a pension with your ex, most companies prefer you to use the so-called fixed date method. Here's how it generally works. Based on your salary and years of service, your benefits office will calculate what your pension would be if you were to retire on the day you expect your divorce to be final. Say you would qualify for a $10,000 pension on that date. A court might order your company to give your spouse $5,000 a year of your pension no matter how big your benefit actually turns out to be when you really retire. Your spouse would start to collect the $5,000 when he or she reaches retirement age (usually 65 though some companies permit earlier retirement) even if you're still working and not receiving your share of the pension.

Some companies let you use a more complicated calculation called the fractional method. Here's how it works. Divide the number of months you were married and employed at your company by the total number of months you've worked for your company, married or not. Next, multiply the result by your estimated pension benefit on the date you plan to retire. Finally, multiply that amount by the percentage of your pension the court has awarded to your spouse. Let's say you've been married 10 years, have worked at your company for 15 years and expect a $20,000 pension when you retire at age 65. Divide 120 by 180 and multiply the result (0.666) by $20,000, resulting in $13,320. If the court gives your spouse half your benefit, he or she would get $6,660 a year. You both take a gamble with this method, however, because you might opt to work beyond 65, thereby boosting your pension and your ex's share of it. If you take early retirement, your pension and your ex's share would be smaller. Whichever method you use, your ex can file for a cut of your pension at the earliest retirement age your company allows. But doing so freezes the amount your ex receives even if you continue to work and your benefits keep growing.

Don't ignore Social Security. An ex may collect up to 50% of the benefit a former spouse has earned when the ex begins receiving Social Security checks. When an ex files for benefits, Social Security automatically compares benefits from his or her own work record with benefits due as an ex-spouse and gives him or her the better deal. To get Social Security benefits as an ex-spouse, you must meet all four of these requirements: 1) your broken marriage must have lasted at least 10 years; 2) you must be 62 or older; 3) your ex must be at least 62 even if he or she isn't retired; 4) you must not be married to a new spouse.

▶ *Picking a Skilled Financial Planner*

As many as 72,000 advisers call themselves financial planners, and 90% claimed in a recent survey that they specialize in retirement planning. Sounds like a buyer's market? Not exactly. Many so-called planners don't know a rollover from a rollaway. But there are also some top-notch planners who can help you reach your goals if you don't feel you can design your own retirement plan. Try first to determine whether you need help from a planner, who is usually a generalist, rather than from a specialist such as an estate lawyer, a C.P.A. or an investment counselor. You need a generalist when you're trying to solve more than one problem involving, say, your company stock options, complex benefit plans and an ex-spouse residing in another state. To find a planner you can trust, you should start by taking these steps.

Identify talented candidates. Ask your accountant, banker or lawyer for recommendations. Or seek names from friends who have used planners and been satisfied with the results. Make sure the candidates have worked in the field for at least three years and use the title C.F.P. (certified financial planner) or Ch.F.C. (chartered financial consultant). To earn either designation, a planner has to take a number of courses in financial fundamentals and pass an exam.

Interview them thoroughly. During an initial meeting, which should be free, ask each planner about his or her experience and the types of services offered. Is the pro well-versed in areas that concern you, such as building a retirement fund or investing for income? Next, ask about payment. There are three types of planners. Fee-only charge about $2,000 to $5,000 for financial plans. Fee-and-commission receive flat fees of $600 or so for plans plus 3% to 5% commissions on investments that you buy from them. And commission-only derive all of their income from the 3% to 5% commissions on investments they sell to you. While salespeople may provide wise counsel, their chief interest is peddling products. Those who earn the bulk of their income selling products may have a conflict of interest that can bias their recommendations. Ask candidates to show you retirement plans for clients with goals and finances that are clearly similar to yours. You should make sure that you understand the plans and that they contain specific investment recommendations such as stocks and mutual funds.

Do a background check. To learn whether your top candidate has been subject to disciplinary actions, call the SEC (202-942-7040) and your state securities department (it's usually part of the Department of Commerce, which is listed in your phone book). If the adviser belongs to the National Association of Securites Dealers, ask the NASD (800-289-9999) whether there have been judgments against him or her for such dubious practices as requiring investment checks to be made out in his or her name rather than to a bank, brokerage or fund company. Once you find a planner that you're comfortable to call your own, your work isn't over. You still need to keep track of your investments and always know what's going on.

▶ *Money's Outlook for Medicare*

The 30-year old Medicare trust fund, the heart of the federal health care program for the elderly, could go bankrupt in 2002. How drastic does the financial cure need to be? The answer is not nearly as severe as the Republican-controlled Congress would lead you to believe. Indeed, MONEY's experts conclude that Medicare, which currently costs the U.S. government $178 billion a year, could get back on its feet if Congress makes several major adjustments. The changes need not be draconian. For instance, we are against the Republican plan to give seniors vouchers to go out and buy their own health coverage. But Medicare's 37 million beneficiaries and the doctors and hospitals that serve them will have to pick up their fair share of the cost of saving the program.

At what cost? Congress wants to slash Medicare spending, which is growing at three times the rate of inflation, by some $260 billion over seven years. That would help Republicans balance the $1.6 trillion federal budget while also delivering some of the tax breaks they promised in the Contract With America. The reality is that only about $150 billion in savings is needed to shore up Medicare. That amount would rescue the hospital insurance trust fund, which is known as Part A and funded by a 2.9% payroll tax. It would also slow the

The Key Elements of Disability Coverage

Have you thought how your life would be upset if you were crippled in an accident? Even if you are nearing retirement, you shouldn't risk going without long-term disability insurance to replace lost income. Viewed as a surrogate paycheck, the policy's benefits should pay out an amount equal to 60% to 80% of your wages. Disability insurance is expensive. A no-frills policy covering 50% of the $75,000 income of a 40-year-old man might start at about $1,000 a year. The price could easily be twice that for a comprehensive plan that, among other things, replaces a higher percentage of income. Before shopping for a policy, check to see what disability coverage you have through your employer—it's usually 20% to 35% cheaper than comparable plans bought on your own. To keep your premium affordable and assure adequate coverage, you want a policy with these features.

▶ **A long waiting period.** Most policies don't start paying benefits until at least 30 days from the date the insurer says you became unable to work. Buying a policy with a 90-day waiting period can save you up to 20% in premiums. If you go out as long as a one-year waiting period, you could save another 11%.

▶ **Benefits paid to age 65.** It's not worth paying 25% more (if you're age 40, for example) to get full lifetime benefits. Pay only for coverage until your retirement age, when Social Security and other savings can be your chief income sources. You also want a policy that can't be canceled and is protected against rate hikes. This is the only way you can be certain that the insurer won't drop your policy or make it unaffordable to you in the future.

▶ **A cost-of-living rider.** Raising your benefits with inflation will jack up premiums 20% to 25%. But you don't want inflation gutting your income when you're out of work. A 40-year-old would pay 14% more in premiums for an automatic 4% annual increase.

▶ **A residual benefit rider.** This lets you work part-time or in a lower-paying job. You then collect the income shortfall, which can total as much as the policy's maximum, from your insurer.

▶ **Own occupation coverage.** You could save about 10% on your premiums with an "any occupation" policy, which pays out only if the insurer determines that you're unable to work anywhere. Instead, you should shop for insurers that offer policies with "own occupation" coverage so that you'll get benefits if you can't do your own job anymore.

rapid growth of Medicare Part B, which is drawn from general tax revenues and beneficiary contributions to cover doctor visits and outpatient services. Searching for a solution that causes the least pain to the elderly, Congress has a selection of savings worth approximately $288 billion that's been dished up by Rep. Christopher Shays (R., Conn.). After reviewing that list, we recommend the following steps toward shoring up Medicare and saving roughly $130 billion.

Make beneficiaries pay more. Today's typical 65-year-old retiree will get back $5.19 in health care benefits over his lifetime for every dollar he paid into the Medicare system. That's a pretty generous payoff and one that could be reduced. Shays figures the government can save $95 billion by the year 2002 by doing the following. First, raise the monthly charge that seniors pay for Part B from $46 to $84, with higher-income folks paying more. (The government would still pay for medical care for the poor). Second, increase the Part B deductible, now $100 a year, to $150 next year and index it to the growth of Medicare spending. And require beneficiaries making 150% above the poverty line ($10,661 for singles and $13,446 for couples) to pay 20% of the cost of lab and home health services, which are now free.

Encourage seniors to join HMOs. Only 9% of Medicare beneficiaries currently are enrolled in HMOs (health maintenance organizations) or other managed care plans, compared with 63% of Americans who have employer-sponsored health insurance. Shays proposes charging new beneficiaries an extra $20 a month, beginning in 1999, if they choose traditional care over a managed care plan. To achieve any real savings, however, Medicare must better manage its managed care arrangements. For instance, the government spends about 6% *more* on seniors who have enrolled in HMOs than it would have if they had stuck with a conventional plan. Medicare officials are working on adjusting the formula they use to pay HMOs. If it can then persuade at least half of all 37 million beneficiaries to join managed care plans, the government could save roughly $2.5 billion a year.

Cut payments to providers. Two ideas could save a total of $35 billion by 2002. First, reduce the generous reimbursement for certain outpatient services, such as ambulatory surgery and diagnostic tests. Second, slow the robust growth of spending on home health care, rehabilitation and skilled nursing care by giving hospitals a single payment covering both in-hospital and post-hospital care. This would eliminate the incentive hospitals now have to discharge patients quickly and send them into home health care settings where reimbursement is unlimited. Once Congress gets Medicare back on its feet, the focus of reform should shift to restructuring the entire health care system. Otherwise doctors and hospitals, both already forced by Medicare to offer services to beneficiaries at discounts, will try to make up lost income by hiking fees for people who are covered by private insurance.

▶ *Your Menu of Medicare Choices*

You become eligible for Medicare at age 65, whether you're retired or employed. You automatically are enrolled if you're receiving Social Security benefits. Otherwise you must sign up at a Social Security office (listed in your phone book). You can enroll within a seven-month period that begins three months before the month in which you turn 65 and ends three months afterwards. Benefits begin immediately. If you miss the window, you will have another chance during the general enrollment period every January through March, and your benefits will start the following July.

Determining the costs you pay. So-called Part A benefits cover care in hospitals, skilled nursing homes, your own home or a hospice for the terminally ill. Part

B benefits pay for outpatient doctor visits and lab fees plus psychiatric and chiropractic services. Part A is free if you've paid FICA taxes for 10 years (not necessarily consecutive). Nonqualifying spouses are eligible once they turn 65. Otherwise you must pay for Part A at a recent rate of $183 a month if you've been employed at least 7.5 years or $261 a month if you've worked less than that. Part A picks up all basic hospital expenses, including medication, semiprivate room and meals, for up to 60 days after you've paid a deductible, lately $716. To get skilled nursing home coverage, you must be hospitalized for at least three days and enter a Medicare-approved facility within 30 days of leaving the hospital. Medicare pays all costs for 20 days.

Part B is optional. You can buy it for a recent $46 monthly premium, an annual $100 deductible and payment of 20% of all covered costs. If you're covered by an employer's or spouse's health plan, however, you should check first to see whether it's a better overall deal. You can always enroll in Part B if your private coverage ends. Note that if you're not covered by an employer's plan, your premium will rise by 10% for each year that you delay signing up.

Figuring how you must pay. After you've paid your 20% share, doctors who participate in Medicare send your bills to the insurance company that serves as your carrier. (For a list of Medicare physicians near you, you should call your state's carrier. A local Social Security office can give you the number.) If you use a nonparticipating doctor, you'll have to pay all charges yourself, then wait a month or so to be reimbursed. Nonparticipating health care providers can't legally charge Medicare recipients more than 115% of Medicare-approved fees. If you join an HMO, Medicare won't charge you Part B deductibles. In return, you usually get free check-ups, eyeglasses and dental care. Note, however, that such services aren't covered by Medicare. For more information on coverage, call 800-772-1213 to request a free copy of the Medicare handbook.

Appealing a disputed claim. If a doctor or hospital tells you that Medicare won't pay for the treatment you need, don't automatically reach for your checkbook. Appeal instead. Only about 2% of Medicare beneficiaries do so. Yet 80% of them win, says Diane Archer of the Medicare Beneficiaries Defense Fund, an advocacy group in New York City. She explains: "Many times doctors and hospitals aren't completely aware of the full range of Medicare coverage." In addition, a recent study by Congress' General Accounting Office indicates that whether you're reimbursed may depend on where you live. Here are two examples. Claims for chest X-rays were 900 times more likely to be denied if processed in Illinois than in neighboring Wisconsin. And payments for certain lab tests were thumbed down 1,400 times more often in Illinois than in California. The chief reason for the disparities seems to be that Medicare claims are handled by more than 30 private insurance companies. (They're called carriers when they deal with hospital claims and intermediaries when they handle outpatient claims.) These companies differ partly because doctors don't always agree about what's medically necessary. Some insurers also review claims more carefully than others and usually tilt in patients' favor. In making an appeal, follow these strategies.

▶ If you question a doctor's judgment that Medicare won't pay for treatment, ask for a written explanation and send it to your carrier for a second opinion.

▶ To challenge a hospital's payment decision, ask its billing office to submit an official claim to the carrier for determination. Or appeal to your local Peer Review Organization, a group of doctors who have contracted with Medicare to settle such disputes. Your hospital's billing office can tell you how to make the appeal.

▶ In disputes about Medicare services at a nursing home or agency involved in home care, you should send a letter explaining your appeal along with your doctor's evaluation of your condition to the Medicare intermediary. (The institution has the address.)

▶ Don't necessarily give up if your first appeal is denied. The official notice that you receive will explain how to carry your battle further. An administrative law judge settles disputes over charges between $100 and $1,000. District courts decide those topping $1,000.

Saving on Medigap policies. New regulations from the Health Care Financing Administration will reduce costs for many people covered by Medicare who must fill gaps in their health insurance. The regulations will correct a problem that Congress inadvertently created in 1990 when it prohibited insurers from selling Medigap policies, which can cost as much as $2,000 a year, to people who already had coverage, usually as part of retirement packages. The legislation, however, had an unexpected result. If your ex-company's policy was among those that only partly supplement Medicare, you couldn't buy coverage to fill in the holes. Instead, you had to drop your ex-employer's policy entirely before acquiring a new one. Thus, if you had free coverage that provided, say, a good drug plan but inadequate reimbursement of co-payments, giving up your employee policy in order to buy a more complete Medigap plan could cost an unnecessary $1,000 a year or more.

The new regulations will let insurance companies sell you the extra coverage after they've given you a pro-forma statement warning that such coverage may duplicate your existing insurance. (Insurers are still prohibited from selling you a second Medigap policy if you already have one.) To find out whether your ex-employer's policy provides all the coverage you need, call your benefits department. Policies that fall short often pay for prescription drugs, eyeglasses or dental care. But they don't pay the deductibles and 20% co-payments for hospital and doctor bills that Medicare doesn't cover. To fill the gaps, you can buy one of 10 standardized Medigap policies, identified by the letters A through J. These

When You Need Medical Help Abroad

If you're worried about what might happen if you become ill when traveling in a foreign country, take the following precautions.

▶ **Do your homework.** For information about vaccinations and health precautions, call the U.S. Center for Disease Control's hotline (404-332-4559). If you do need pretrip care, get it from a doctor who specializes in travel medicine. For a free list, send a stamped, self-addressed envelope to Dr. Leonard Marcus, Traveler's Health and Immunization Service, 148 Highland Ave., Newton, Mass. 02160.

▶ **Line up help in advance.** For $75, plus $1 a day for the length of your trip, Global Emergency Medical Services (800-860-1111) will give you access to a 24-hour hotline, staffed by nurses who can help determine, say, whether you need hospitalization to treat your diarrhea or only Immodium-D, an inexpensive antidote. Want a retired nurse to travel with you? Call the Traveling Nurses Network through the Disability Bookshop (800-637-2256). Referrals cost $10, and many nurses are willing to trade care for travel costs.

▶ **Check out your insurance.** Ask your agent whether your existing policy covers overseas emergencies. To close gaps, you can buy an inexpensive travel policy. Virtually all such policies pay health care charges in advance, which foreign hospitals often demand, and cover evacuation costs. TravMed, for example, recently offered couples $100,000 in coverage for $3.15 a day if they're under age 70 ($5 a day if 70 to 80). TravMed also provides 24-hour, toll-free assistance to help you find a doctor or hospital. You and your spouse can obtain a month's coverage (evacuation, up-front hospital costs and $15,000 in insurance) for $142 from TravelAssistance International (800-821-2828). In addition, its 24-hour, toll-free number can put you in touch with physicians at George Washington University Hospital in Washington, D.C., who will help guide foreign caregivers.

▶ **What to do in a pinch overseas.** If you need immediate medical assistance, call the local American embassy or consulate. All can provide physician referrals. American Express cardholders can make collect calls to the firm's Global Assist service (301-214-8228) for the names of physicians who trained in the U.S. and speak English. Visa (401-581-9994) and MasterCard (303-278-800) also offer 24-hour medical assistance but only to Gold Card holders (call collect). MasterCard Business Card holders are covered for evacuation costs up to $10,000 plus $2,500 in medical insurance with a $50 deductible.

range from bare-bones insurance that pays only for those 20% co-payments to ones also covering skilled nursing care, at-home recovery, 50% of all prescription drug costs and preventive care.

Every insurer offers the same plans but at different prices. You can get descriptions of the plans from the Medicare-Medigap Counseling office of your state insurance department (the number is in your phone book). Once you determine your need, don't forget to shop around for the best price. And remember to compare how prices will rise as you age.

▶ The Top Deals in Health Insurance

Medical insurance remains the No. 1 problem for early retirees. Today, retired people in their late fifties must pay up to $5,000 a year for comprehensive health insurance until they reach age 65 and qualify for Medicare. This assumes both spouses don't smoke and are in good health. What's more, former employers are increasingly unwilling to pick up part of the tab. If your ex-employer doesn't offer adequate coverage, there are ways to make private coverage more affordable. If you need help, you can hire a professional service such as Wilkinson's Benefit Consultants (800-296-3030) to scour its database of nearly 1,000 carriers for the three plans that suit you best. Or call Quotesmith (800-556-9393) for 60 to 70 quotes from various carriers. That's a lot of choices. But the data are free because member insurance companies pay the fee. Here's our advice.

Buy only coverage you need. In general, a comprehensive policy should pay most doctor bills in full or in part plus the full cost of hospitalization and surgery (once you've met a deductible and any co-payment). The policy should also cover bills for catastrophic care (up to at least $500,000) and part of your costs for prescription drugs and home-based health care. To be sure your insurance will be there when you need it, you should buy a policy from a company rated A or A+ for financial soundness by A.M. Best (available in most libraries). You can reduce a premium by increasing your deductible, co-payment or stop loss (the sum at which the insurer begins to pay 100% of your costs). A typical individual plan with a $250 deductible costs around $515 a month. The same coverage with a $1,000 deductible costs about $390 a month. You can also save by cutting costly policy features you don't need, such as maternity coverage at $100 to $150 a month. Whichever policy you buy, make sure it's guaranteed renewable so it can't be canceled if your health takes a bad turn.

Check out group rates. Group coverage is sometimes cheaper than individual policies. Premiums vary with the type of plan, the number and age of the group's members and their general health. For instance, the 250,000-member National Organization for Women, which any man or woman can join for $35 a year, offers couples of any age comprehensive coverage from Banker's Life & Casualty for about $470 a month. If you own your own business or are self-employed, you also can buy group coverage. Unless you're pooled with thousands of people, however, you may not get an attractive rate. And group plans are required by many states to include a number of mandatory coverages such as pregnancy that older people may not want to pay for.

Think COBRA for chronic illness. If you have a serious problem such as cancer or back pain, your best insurance bet may be to stick with your company's medical plan as long as you can. The federal Consolidated Omnibus Budget Reconciliation Act (COBRA) gives you 60 days from the day you stop working to decide whether to keep your old coverage for up to 18 months. One strategy is to keep your company plan and buy a private policy. That way you'll be protected during the six to 12 months you must wait before the new policy covers your pre-existing condition. But the price probably will be stiff. COBRA costs at least $5,200 a year. Kentucky,

Maine, New Hampshire, New Jersey, New York, Vermont and Washington require insurers offering individual policies to cover anyone regardless of health after a waiting period of as long as a year. Most other states insist that small group policies be available to anyone. As a last resort, ask your state insurance commissioner (the number is in your phone book) whether your state has a high-risk pool offering coverage to anyone. The premium is often 25% to 50% above standard rates.

Consider joining an HMO. Group HMO plans cost at least 13% less than most traditional indemnity plans. In addition, there's a fee of $5 to $10 each time you visit the doctor and $2 to $5 for each prescription. Unlike traditional plans, HMOs cover routine physical exams and other preventive services. One drawback is that you can't choose your doctor unless your HMO offers a feature called point of service. This extra lets you see doctors who aren't members of your HMO, usually for a 30% co-payment. But it may also boost your premium by approximately 5%. Managed care alternatives that are commonly called preferred provider organizations (PPOs) let you choose from a list of participating physicians for roughly the same cost as HMOs with an option for point of service.

▶ *How to Find the Best HMO for You*

In the past five years, the number of Medicare beneficiaries who have signed up with HMOs has doubled. The allure is easy to appreciate. By joining an HMO, you receive all of Medicare's services without having to pay extra charges including deductibles that run as high as $800 a year, 20% co-payments for outpatient services or most costs for prescription drugs. In addition, HMOs offer vision, dental and preventive care that Medicare doesn't cover. The cost can be as much as $100 a month, on top of Medicare's standard $46 premium.

If you're tempted to sign up, you should first ask your present doctor whether he or she works with an HMO. By joining that one, you won't have to switch to a doctor on the HMO's approved list, a requirement of all HMOs. This so-called primary care physician (PCP) will oversee your medical care and authorize any services from specialists or hospitals. You'll have to pay higher costs if you want to see a doctor outside of the HMO's network or feel there's treatment you need and your PCP doesn't concur.

If your doctor doesn't work with an HMO, seek recommendations from friends who belong to one or call your state's insurance department for a list of Medicare HMOs in your area. The department can also tell you about complaints on file regarding an HMO. One potential problem is that most HMOs pay doctors according to the number of patients they care for, not according to the number of services they provide. Critics charge that this system encourages doctors to see lots of patients but give them little attention. Some HMOs also pay their PCPs additional income at the end of the year if they haven't referred patients to costly specialists. If you disagree with your doctor's decision regarding treatment or if an HMO refuses to pay for emergency care, you can appeal. (The HMO will tell you how to do it.) Once you've identified a likely HMO, call to interview a representative and get answers to the following questions.

▶ What benefits does the HMO offer besides those that are covered by Medicare? Expect at least check-ups, eyeglasses, dental care and prescription drugs.

▶ How long must you wait to see your physician? Don't settle for longer than a day or two if you're mildly sick and two weeks for a check-up.

▶ How much do I pay for someone unaffiliated with the HMO? A small number of HMOs charge members a deductible of $100 or so and a co-payment of at least 50%. Most others make you pay full price.

If what you learn about the HMO makes you comfortable, interview up to three of its physicians. Ask whether they can be reached easily by phone, day or night, and whether they like the HMO's hospitals and specialists. A sympatico physician should also ask you about your medical history and concerns. What happens if you join an HMO and subsequently become dissatisfied? You can drop out at any time, either by certified letter to the HMO or by completing Form 566 at a Social Security office. You'll still be protected by Medicare's regular coverage.

▶ Sign These Key Documents Now

Nobody likes to think about the possibility of one day becoming incapacitated. Yet the time to write down your wishes for medical treatment is while you're still in good health. Here are documents that you will need.

A living will specifies your wishes for medical treatment if you become terminally ill and thus unable to communicate with your doctor. Trouble is, doctors can easily disregard a living will. So you should also sign a durable power of attorney for health care. This document names a person as your proxy to make medical decisions on your behalf, including hiring or firing a doctor. Your proxy can act anytime you're unconscious, not just when you're terminally ill. The living will effectively acts as a guide for your proxy, giving him or her greater conviction when faced with a difficult decison. And you don't need a lawyer to draft either document. Give copies to your proxy, doctor and family.

A durable power of attorney, which should be drafted by a lawyer, names a person to oversee your financial affairs when you're incapacitated. Pick your agents carefully because they can do a great deal of harm. For peace of mind, you might consider naming two agents and require signatures from both for all transactions. Or you could limit your agent's access to certain accounts. If you want your agent to deal with Social Security or the IRS, you must specify your wishes in the document.

Index